Every Woman's Journey

The Silver Wheel reveals the primal archetypes deep within every woman. Uncover the influences at work within your life and learn how to awaken the hidden aspects of your innermost self. Journey to the Otherworld and bring back your own guardian spirit. Discover the warning signs of being emotionally drawn to the darker recesses of the Otherworld. Renew your inner strength, sense of purpose, and identity through the powerful techniques of shamanism.

Hear the voice of your own wise counsel. Learn to discriminate between which relationships are healthy and which ones are not. End the tug of war between personal contentment and compromise in your life. Become your own lover and recognize the Demon Lover as the inner god in every woman's soul. *The Silver Wheel* is your guide to magical empowerment and spiritual re-awakening.

Through myth and legend, visualization and imagination, you will experience a revelation of the mysteries awaiting each woman who sets out upon the starry road of the Silver Wheel—the path of personal transformation.

About the Authors

Marguerite Elsbeth is a professional astrologer and Tarot reader with more than twenty years experience. She has published many articles in magazines such as Dell's *Horoscope* and *The Mountain Astrologer*. A hereditary strega, she is also proud of her Delaware Indian ancestry.

Kenneth Johnson holds a degree in comparative religions with an emphasis on the study of mythology. Born in Southern California, he has lived in Los Angeles, Amsterdam, London, and New Mexico.

To Write to the Authors

If you wish to contact the authors or would like more information about this book, please write to the authors in care of Llewellyn Worldwide, and we will forward your request. Both the authors and the publisher appreciate hearing from you and learning of your enjoyment of this book and how it has helped you. Llewellyn Worldwide cannot guarantee that every letter written to the authors can be answered, but all will be forwarded. Please write to:

Marguerite Elsbeth and Kenneth Johnson
⁒ Llewellyn Worldwide
P.O. Box 64383, Dept. K371–9
St. Paul, MN 55164-0383, U.S.A.
Please enclose a self-addressed, stamped envelope for reply or $1.00 to cover costs.
If outside the U.S.A., enclose international postal reply coupon.

Free Llewellyn Catalog

For more than ninety years, Llewellyn has brought its readers knowledge in the fields of metaphysics and human potential. Learn about the newest books in spiritual guidance, natural healing, astrology, occult philosophy, and more. Enjoy book reviews, New Age articles, a calendar of events, plus current advertised products and services. To get your free copy of *Llewellyn's New Worlds*, send your name and address to:

Llewellyn's New Worlds of Mind and Spirit
P.O. Box 64383, Dept K371–9, St. Paul, MN 55164-0383, U.S.A.

LLEWELLYN'S CELTIC WISDOM SERIES

The
Silver
Wheel

WOMEN'S MYTHS & MYSTERIES
IN THE CELTIC TRADITION

Marguerite Elsbeth &
Kenneth Johnson

1997
Llewellyn Publications
St. Paul, Minnesota 55164-0383, U.S.A.

FIRST EDITION
Second Printing, 1997

Cover design: Anne Marie Garrison
Cover art: Carrie Westfall
Interior illustrations: Nyease Merlin Somersett
Book design, layout, and editing: Jessica Thoreson

Library of Congress Cataloging-in-Publication Data
Elsbeth, Marguerite, 1953–
    The silver wheel: women's myths & mysteries in the Celtic tradition /
    Marguerite Elsbeth & Kenneth Johnson. — 1st ed.
        p.   cm. — (Llewellyn's Celtic wisdom series)
    Companion volume to: The Grail Castle / Kenneth Johnson.
    Includes bibliographical references.
    ISBN 1-56718-371-9 (trade paperback)
    1. Goddess religion. 2. Women—Religious life. 3. Mythology,
    Celtic. 4. New Age movement. I. Johnson, Kenneth, 1952–   .
    II. Johnson, Kenneth, 1952–   Grail Castle. III. Title. IV. Series.
    BL473.5.E47   1996
    299'.93—dc20   96-43652

Llewellyn Publications
A Division of Llewellyn Worldwide, Ltd.
P.O. Box 64383, Dept. K371–9, St. Paul, MN 55164-0383

About Llewellyn's Celtic Wisdom Series

Can it be said that we are all Celts? Western civilization owes as much, if not more, to our Celtic heritage as to Greek and Roman influences.

While the origins of the Celtic peoples are shrouded in the mists of time, they seem to have come from central Europe in the first millenium B.C., moving out across Europe and occupying areas from Asia Minor to Spain, France, and finally Scotland and Ireland.

Basic to the Celtic tradition is the acceptance of personal responsibility and realization that all of us constantly shape and affect the land on which we live. Intrinsic to this notion is the Celtic interrelationship with the Otherworld and its inhabitants. The Celtic world view is a magical one, in which everything has a physical, mental, and spiritual aspect and its own proper purpose, and where our every act affects both worlds.

The books of the Celtic Wisdom Series comprise a magical curriculum embracing ideas and techniques that awaken the soul to the myths and legends, the psychological and spiritual truths, and the inner power each of us can tap to meet the challenges of our times.

Other Books by Marguerite Elsbeth and Kenneth Johnson:

The Grail Castle: Male Myths & Mysteries in the Celtic Tradition

Other Books by Marguerite Elsbeth:

FORTHCOMING

Crystal Medicine

Other Books by Kenneth Johnson:

Mythic Astrology: Archetypal Powers in the Horoscope (with Ariel Guttman)
North Star Road: Shamanism, Witchcraft & the Otherworld Journey
Jaguar Wisdom: Mayan Calendar Magic

FORTHCOMING

Pagan Slavic Sorcery

Acknowledgements

We would like to remember the individuals who wove their way in and through the tapestry of our lives while we wrote this book, and then some:

The following women are Goddesses in their own right: Sandra Weschcke, Nancy J. Mostad, Anne Marie Garrison, Nyease Merlin Somersett, Jessica Thoreson, Christine Le May Spindler, Sandra Reading Kadisak, Anna Huserik, Leise Sargent, Ellen Millington, Barbara Gage, Shahin Medghalchi, Fredda Willis Rizzo, and Sandra Hughes.

While the following men are Champions of the Goddess, all: Carl Llewellyn Weschcke, Richard Kinsey, Neil Hassel, Robert "Dude" Perry, Michael Spindler, Michael Hickey, Michael Kadisak, Mark Mrus, and Jay Mrus.

Table of Contents

PART I

EMERGENCE

CHAPTER ONE

The Meeting with Rhiannon

We emerge into individualized consciousness gradually, though there are certain moments that constitute rites of passage, initiations into the game of life....

*T*HE MAIDEN APPEARED *on the mound called Gorsedd Arberth. The night was bright with stars, the weather calm and fair, and the horse she rode whiter than the snowy peaks of the distant mountains. Her horse trod the ground at an even pace. As she came up the path, she saw the band of men sitting in the distance. She was in no hurry to meet them, nor was she afraid.*

The maiden drew closer to the warriors perched on the mound, her garment of shining gold-brocaded silk a glimmering halo about her slender form, her face covered with a veil. One of the men arose at the command of Pwyll, Prince of Dyved, who had been sitting on the mound with his men, waiting to see a wonder. The man stepped onto the path to meet the maiden, but she had already traveled past. He followed her as fast as he could on foot, but the faster he walked, the more he fell behind. Meanwhile, the maiden neither hastened nor slowed her pace.

When the man gave his report to Pwyll, the prince sent him back to court for the swiftest horse in Dyved and ordered him to ride after the maiden. The man spurred his horse to action, galloping at full speed along the path in pursuit of the beautiful woman. The maiden and her horse gleamed in the silver moonlight and remained just out of reach, ahead on the trail. Finally the warrior realized it was futile to spur his tired horse onward in hopes of catching her.

He returned to Pwyll and told his story. Pwyll declared that the maiden obviously had a message for them, but was too stubborn to state her purpose. The men returned to court for their evening meat.

On the following day, Pwyll asked his men to accompany him once again to the top of the mound to sit. After a short while, the maiden appeared in the distance on her pale white horse, her golden finery shining all about her. She came toward them at an even pace. This time Pwyll was ready, his own horse saddled and waiting at the side of the road. But no sooner had he gained his mount than she passed him by.

Pwyll's horse pranced and danced and took off after the maiden at lightning-swift speed. Surely he would catch up to her. But try as he might, the deeper he dug his spurs into the broad, now-bloodied flanks of his horse, and the faster his horse ran, he was no nearer to her than before.

Finally, exasperated and exhausted, Pwyll spoke. "Maiden, for the sake of whomever you love best, please wait for me."

The maiden said, "Gladly I will wait, and it would have been better for the horse if you had asked me sooner."

The night was bright with stars, the weather calm and fair, and the horse she rode whiter than the snowy peaks of the distant mountains ....

She drew back the veil of her headdress, revealing a fine, delicately featured face. She fixed her gaze upon Pwyll and began to converse with him. He inquired as to her origin and where she might be going.

"I have things to accomplish," she replied, "but I'm glad to see you."

As Pwyll gazed upon her lovely countenance, he was smitten by her beauty and believed that every woman he had ever seen was unlovely by comparison. "Lady," he said, "won't you please tell me of your errands?"

"My main errand was to try to see you," she answered.

Pwyll expressed his pleasure at her response, and then asked, "Will you tell me who you are?"

"I will," said she. "I am Rhiannon, daughter of Heveydd the Old, and I am being married against my will. I have not wished for a husband because I love you; I will not have him as my husband even if you reject me. I have come to this place to hear your answer."

Pwyll said, "This is my answer to you—that if I could choose among all the women in the world, I would choose you."

To this she replied, "If this is what you want, then before I am given to another man, make a tryst with me."

"The sooner the better," said Pwyll.

So Rhiannon set a tryst that one year from that day, at the court of Heveydd, she would have a feast prepared in readiness for Pwyll's coming. After bidding him farewell and admonishing him to keep his promise, they parted company for the time being....

Rhiannon bursts onto the pages of the old Welsh story collection we call the *Mabinogion*[1] just like a young woman bursting onto the stage of life. She is just beginning her journey down the path of experience, of consciousness. All of us, women and men alike, emerge from the great ocean of the collective mind, the ocean of human experience which is comprised of so many elements—our heritage, our culture, our families, and our karma. This great collective mind—which Carl Jung called the collective unconscious—contains within it all the actors and actresses who take part in that great drama we call our lives. In order to play the leading lady on the stage of her own life, a woman must emerge from the collective and become a true individual. This is what Rhiannon does when she bursts forth out of the faery mound.

In Ireland, the Neolithic burial mounds that dot the landscape were (and sometimes still are) called the "houses of the *sidhe.*" Who are the *sidhe?* They are the faery folk, the inhabitants of the Otherworld. But the beings whom country people call the faery folk are none other than the ancient goddesses and gods, the true inhabitants of our inner collective sea. It is from this enchanted realm, the realm of childhood where all things are merged into one and our perceptions are pure and open, that Rhiannon emerges and begins her road.

But the road itself—where does it lead?

Women and men walk different roads, and this is as it should be, for it is part of the cosmic duality of life. Many of the world's mystical traditions affirm that we live in a universe alive with polarity. Our world is a dynamic symphony of opposites. One way to define these opposites is in terms of male and female. Most often, however, different spiritual traditions find their own names for it: the Chinese perceive these eternal dualities as yin (female) and yang (male), while Tantric Hindus personify them as Shiva (male) and Shakti (female). In some of our own Western traditions, they are defined as active (male) and passive (female), although these words may sound unacceptable to some women, for they would seem to imply a value judgment.

Indeed, countless cultural and metaphysical difficulties have arisen on this planet from trying to make a value judgment between two principles which are, in the end, complementary. Christianity, Judaism, and Islam, for example, have had the nasty habit of equating most masculine qualities with light, and therefore with "good," while feminine qualities have been historically perceived as dark, therefore "evil." Unfortunately, many women, in an attempt to restore for themselves a sense of worthiness and an appreciation of the feminine side of existence, simply reverse the polarities, defining the feminine principle as "good" and the masculine principle as "bad." This is essentially no different than the way Christians and Muslims think. An appreciation of both polarities is necessary for health and spiritual growth, and nothing teaches this appreciation quite like the mystery of our human relationships.

Carl Jung drew upon ancient Greek (especially Hermetic) writings in defining the masculine or yang principle as *logos* and the feminine or yin principle as *eros*. The Greek word *logos* is related to our word "logic," and it implies that man's natural path is to wield the sword of the mind. Like all other mortals, men too emerge from the great womb of the unconscious, the Great Mother's barrow mound of the soul wherein all things are birthed. But it is man's destiny to become separate, to learn to discriminate. Thus, in time, he divides the world into discrete entities, black and white, for this is what a warrior must do. In male myths, the collective unconscious, the childhood state, is often seen as a great forest where the hero grows up orphaned. He is dwarfed and lost in the great depths. Then he pulls his sword from its scabbard and cuts his way through the forest until he reaches his destination. He moves always in a straight line. He remembers the unity of all things only as a dream—the all-encompassing forest from which he has emerged, or the mysterious Grail Castle which appears like magic in the midst of a knight's quest. If he is wise, if he travels far enough on his road, he may someday re-enter the Grail Castle of the dream, and find a new, mystic sense of unity—this, after all, is what it means to find the Holy Grail. But unless he is an artist or a seer, he will never dwell for any length of time in the great Otherworld of dreams and collective memories.

Women, however, never quite lose their sense of unity. The principle of *eros* refers, of course, to "love," and to love something—anything—means to desire union with it, to embrace it both sexually and spiritually. Thus a woman always retains one foot in the great barrow mound of Gorsedd Arberth—she is always aware that, in the end, we are not separate from the universe around us, but bound to it with chains of love, chains which are (to use the Greek term again) erotic. So relating is what a woman does best, whether she relates to her mother, father, child, a man, or to the cosmos.

Thus a woman's road, unlike a man's, is circular. Her path will wind back to where it began. Emerging from the world of dreams, she will someday return to it, for she is in essence a creature of the Otherworld, and must return on occasion to rejuvenate herself and gain her share of women's wisdom. This, at least, is what the great myths and legends of the world tell us, for our deep unconscious images of the feminine are all circular.

This circular path has been imaged in many different forms. To many traditional peoples, the wheel of the year itself was the body of the Goddess going through its transformations. Thus the ancient Celts fashioned images of the Goddess on St. Brigid's Day, February 2, the ancient feast of Imbolc. They laid the image or "corn dolly" in a cradle, as if the Goddess and the season of spring were being born beneath the earth, while the world lay in its deepest winter sleep. On Beltane or May Day, the rich burgeoning of spring was celebrated with maypoles and sensual license, and at Midsummer the flames of the bonfires leapt high to honor the turning of the yearly tide, the beginning of the shorter days. On August 2 or Lammastide, the first fruits of the harvest were offered up in the name of Lugh, lover and son of the Goddess. Then, on Samhain—what we call Halloween—the world turned toward winter and the spirits of dead ancestors drew closer, cracking the doors between the worlds. At Midwinter, the bonfires were lit again as the days began to lengthen.

Traditional peoples have always recognized a correspondence between earth and sky—a correspondence which found its way into later Hermetic philosophy in the form of the famous axiom "As above, so below." Thus the earthly wheel of the year must have its metaphor in the heavens. In fact, every portion of the starry sky—the slow rising and setting of the constellations as well as the progress of the sun and moon—was symbolic of some spiritual, psychological, or mystical truth. To Druidic astronomers, the constellation we now call Corona Borealis, the Northern Crown, was the castle of Arianrhod, the Lady of the Silver Wheel.

For now, let us follow Rhiannon as she rides on everywoman's journey, the spiraling path around the Silver Wheel....

We emerge into individualized consciousness gradually, though there are certain moments that constitute rites of passage, initiations into the game of life. One of these moments is the onset of puberty, and we might compare Rhiannon, bursting forth from the Otherworld, to a young girl on the threshold of womanhood. Though she has traveled a decade or more since birth, her real entrance into the world will begin when the blood coursing through her veins becomes visible in the outer world and she becomes capable of bearing children.

In many cultures, puberty is a time when a young woman must be secluded, neither touching the ground nor seeing the sun. In some traditional cultures of Africa, Oceania, and North America, it was believed that if she walked upon the earth the crops would wither and fail, the wine would turn to vinegar, mirrors would dim, metals would rust, and horses would miscarry. If her gaze turned toward the sun, she might become pregnant. She was taboo—unclean, infectious, a polluted vessel capable of condemning men to failure or even death. Her body was thought to be weak and unhealthy, her temperament unstable. There was yet another reason a pubescent maiden was doomed to isolation and confinement: she had reached her power time, her divinity; the supernatural hovered close by. Men feared the light as much as they feared the darkness. To neutralize that power, the energy capable of bringing life, death, and rebirth, a girl was sent away, excluded, suspended between heaven and earth.[2]

A part of this mysterious process is mirrored in Rhiannon's tale. She appears on the mound of Gorsedd Arberth riding a horse, her face covered by a veil. She neither touches the ground nor sees the sun. Pwyll and his men cannot gaze upon her face as she passes them by. Yet they are intrigued by the undulating movement of her lithe golden form. Pwyll and his men had been waiting to "see a wonder," and indeed they have seen one: the power of a woman newly born.

Though the story itself seems to comprise a span of only a few days, we may wonder whether an entire process in everywoman's life is implied—a process that, in fact, extends over several years. Although the *Mabinogion* contains a great deal of ancient Celtic mythology, the earliest manuscript we possess dates only from the thirteenth century. Christian monks and medieval storytellers had already worked centuries of "improvements" on the old Pagan material, and one may speculate freely as to the original mythic purpose of the tales. When Rhiannon emerges from the mound, she is, at least symbolically, much like a girl who has just entered puberty, the first preovulatory phase of menstruation when the ovarian follicles ripen and mature. As the chase continues into the story's second day, she has symbolically experienced the ovulatory phase when the ripe egg is expelled from the ovary, followed by the premenstrual phase when the estrogen and progesterone levels drop. Finally, she will have entered the menstrual phase itself, when the womb lining is shed and the blood begins to pour down.[3]

No wonder, then, that Rhiannon pays no heed to Pwyll on the first day. She is still in seclusion. It is upon the "second day" of the story that Rhiannon at last stops for Pwyll's beseeching words, conversing with him, revealing herself to him, and finally announcing her intention to marry him. This aspect of courtship, which we shall soon explore in more detail, corresponds to the postmenstrual phase.

There exists a special connection between the four phases of menstruation and the twenty-eight day cycle of the moon, for there are also four phases to the lunar cycle—waxing, full, waning, and the dark or new moon. These lunar phases outline a rhythm which is deeply rooted in a woman's physical experience.[4] Ideally, this rhythm should flow in harmony with nature, the sum total of all things in time and space, and the entire physical universe, including the plants and animals that are a part of it. This must also include a woman's own inner nature, her inborn character, innate disposition, and inherent tendencies, as well as the vital functions, forces, and activities of the organs in her physical body. When a woman is not in tune with the corporeal aspect of her life-experience, she becomes prone to all manner of physical, emotional, mental, and spiritual discomfort.

Although the menses, the outpouring of blood from the chalice of a woman's uterus, has long been viewed as deadly to men, the chalice itself has been much sought after. The cup which, in Celtic myth, sometimes goes by the name of the Holy Grail has been equated with the womb of the Goddess, and only its contents can heal the ailing Grail King whose world has become blighted. What, then, fills the Grail? Life-force, blood, the very essence of the soul.

Though blood was feared, it was also deemed a preserving and protecting fluid, capable of soothing the soul and returning the soul to the body. In order to protect themselves in battle, the Gauls—Celtic inhabitants of pre-Roman France—would drink and paint themselves with the blood of their enemies.

Their antagonists, the Romans, took a different tack: in order to ensure good crops, the best horse in the area was sacrificed to the god Mars. The creature was stabbed with a spear, and its head and tail cut off and adorned. These items were taken to the king's house and the blood from them allowed to drip into the hearth. The rest of the blood coming from the horse's body was caught and preserved for use in purifying the cattle in the spring.

The close link between the horse and the concept of sacred blood brings us back to Rhiannon's emergence. She is riding a horse, and the horse has a mythological significance of great power. It is wind, seafoam, light, and fire—the ether of cosmic force bursting forth from the primordial darkness, instigating creation in the vastnesses of space, seeding earth, igniting passion in the heart of humankind. The horse is associated with natural desire and instinct, for, after all, it has a moon-shaped hoof. The moon is symbolic of emotions, feelings, responses, the mother, and of women in general; also of memory, nurturance, and change. According to astrology, the moon holds sway over our moods and habits; it is at the root of sensitivity, emotionalism, intuition, sentimentality, self-protection, and everything that equals "home." The term "lunatic" aptly describes an overwrought, emotionally disturbed temperament. Many women experience overwhelming emotions when they are premenstrual, and some might go so far as to say that they are always in a bad mood—being either premenstrual, menstrual, postmenstrual, or ovulating!

The lunar faculties of cyclic movement, and of phenomena such as divination and clairvoyance, are also associated with the horse, which is a psychic and sensitive creature in its own right. Carl Jung correlates the horse with mother and intuition, basic instinctual energy, and the element of water. The horse has always been an especially powerful animal or "totem" for women, and especially at the time of puberty. How many girls of this age spend their time drawing pictures of horses on their school notebooks, lost in a dream and unaware of whatever the teacher is droning on about?

The horse has been a sacred animal in Britain since prehistoric times, and its gigantic image is carved in chalk on the side of a hill near Uffington. Throughout the British Isles, there has always been a taboo against eating horse-flesh.[5] The English associate the white horse with death and burial rites as well. This reminds us of the link between the horse and the Roman god Mars, who as god of battles is also symbolic of death, transformation, and regeneration. That Rhiannon emerges from the Otherworld mounted upon a horse who symbolizes death indicates that she has undergone the feminine process which leads to rebirth, that she has left her former self, her childhood, behind.

It is likely that Rhiannon, in most ancient times, was herself a white horse, for it has been speculated that she is the same as the Gallo-Roman goddess Epona, depicted as a woman astride a horse.[6] In fact, the epiphany of the Goddess on the horse seems to have been a fairly common one in the British Isles. In a May Eve festival, a woman was chosen to portray the Goddess—emerging like the spring—and to ride naked through the countryside. This ritual is commemorated in the well-known British folktale of Lady Godiva, who, it may be remembered, rode naked through the streets of Coventry. One man—the original "peeping Tom"—was struck blind because he gazed upon her. No man may behold the divine face of the Goddess in all her glory and live to tell about it, which suggests yet another reason that Rhiannon's face is veiled.

Every woman, then, must emerge from the womb-world of the mother into a sense of individuality, and puberty is the age-old symbol of that rite of passage, that emergence. For too many women, especially in the Western world, this is a confusing time. Braces, pimples, and general awkwardness prevail over glory, and a lack of acceptable outlets for burgeoning sexual energy make the issues more painful yet. But myth teaches us that the moment of emergence should be powerful and passionate rather than awkward and introverted. A young woman should shine with the light of the Goddess within. Lifting the reins of sexual power and riding it like a horse, she stays one step ahead of boys the same age, who are developing somewhat more slowly. Try as they might, they cannot catch up with her, nor can they touch her, for the moment of her leap into individuality has endowed her with an Otherworldly glow, something that is not quite earthly and hence not quite accessible. She has arisen from the faery mound, still garbed in the glorious colors of the Otherworld. This, of course, is the moment when it is pscyhologically and spiritually appropriate for a boy or young man to worship the Goddess within her—he may learn to take her seriously as a human being a bit later on. Unfortunately, our concept of relationships in the Western world is in itself rather adolescent, and most of us—men and women alike—never quite get beyond the fascination with either worshipping the inaccessible or being worshipped as such. Rhiannon herself will have to confront that issue during the next phase of her journey.

All women walk the starry road of the Silver Wheel, which circles ever round and round, back to where it first began. Most women walk it in three stages, which we call Maiden, Mother, and Crone. As we know, everything on earth has its reflection in the stars, and these three phases of a woman's life have their correspondence in the three phases of the moon. Although the moon, as we know, technically has four phases, mythically she has three. She waxes as Maiden, reaches fullness as a Mother or a Queen, and wanes into the dark wisdom of the Crone.

The ancients saw the cycle of the moon as a dance in three phases, but they also recognized that the circle of life may be divided into four parts. Indeed, Jung believed that even numbers were essentially "feminine" while odd numbers were "masculine." The gods of the patriarchal Indo-Europeans were organized into triads—as was the Christian deity, which was perceived as a trinity. Earth-centered faiths, on the other hand, organize their universe into a fourfold scheme—the best-known such system is probably the Native American Medicine Wheel, with its four sacred directions. This fourfold division of reality may also put us in mind of the four seasons and the four great seasonal festivals of the Celtic peoples—Imbolc, Beltane, Lammas, and Samhain, as described above. It is also worth noting that occult philosophy of the medieval and Renaissance periods—which formed an underground stream flowing in the opposite direction from orthodox Christianity—retained this fourfold cosmos in the form of the four elements of alchemy and astrology.

The fourfold cosmos, however, is much older than the Middle Ages—older even than the Celtic world from which the story of Rhiannon emerged. The cross of the four directions can be found on pottery from southeastern Europe that dates back to about 5000 B.C. The cultures that produced this pottery were centered in peaceful, agricultural villages that appear to have been matriarchal or matrilineal in nature. This, of course, is the so-called "Goddess Era" of the Neolithic.

According to Jung, the four directions or four elements express themselves within all of us, women and men alike, as four distinct functions of the psyche—intuition, feeling, thinking, and sensation. We can also think of this mysterious fourfold orientation in terms of personality types. These four personalities were first identified by a female psychologist, Toni Wolff, and applied to feminine psychology.[7] They can just as easily be applied to masculine psychology, and indeed some writers (including the present authors) have done so.[8]

All women contain all four of these personality types within them; there is no such thing as a "pure" type. However, for reasons of family

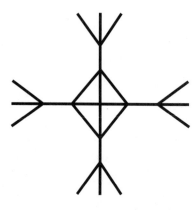

Figure 1: The Cross of the Four Directions

upbringing, personal preference, or pure and simple destiny, one or two types may tend to dominate over the others. These four types can be described as follows:

The first, and most primal, manifestation of the feminine is the **Mother,** although it might be best to call her the **Queen** when dealing with Celtic myth, for the Queen was the Mother of the Land, and the old Welsh and Irish tales are rich with such queens. She is oriented toward the outer world, and tends to focus her attention on shelter and security. Because she is so deeply oriented towards society's goals, she may tend to see men as objects rather than individuals—a man is valued in terms of his role as father, provider, and caretaker. In other words, the Queen is the type of woman most likely to do what advocates of the men's movement accuse so many women of doing—regarding men as purely financial objects, suitable only for bringing home the bacon and working on the car. In similar fashion, the Queen expects her children to play out their allotted social roles and become doctors, lawyers—or the faithful wives of such exalted figures. The Queen's essential urge is to protect: in myth, she protects the land, and in modern life she seeks to protect the family and the home. At her worst, she can be over-protective, and—a word often applied to mothers—downright meddlesome. At her best, she is the personification of the great nurturing warmth of all nature.

If the Queen seeks to rule in the daylight realm of the outer world, the **Medium** finds her natural domain in the depths of the great collective barrow mound of the soul. Some Jungians call this personality type the

Sibyl or Norn; in Celtic terms, we might best name her the **Sorceress.** She is thoroughly immersed in the subjective realm of psychic perception, and it is in the world of that inner perception that her greatest strengths and weaknesses lie. She is aware of the cosmic intangibles of human life; and yet she may be oblivious to everyday reality and its demands, both practical and emotional. If she is wise, she may serve those around her as a source of true feminine wisdom, a channel of communication between the bright world of sun and sky and the deep world of the collective barrow mound which is lit only by flickering elf-lights. But if she is undeveloped, she may come to regard her own personal intuitions as cosmic truths, which all and sundry must obey—and if she herself is in great but unacknowledged personal turmoil, this is a dangerous path indeed, for not only does it misguide others, it opens the Sorceress herself up to dark psychic forces.

The third type was named the **Amazon** by Dr. Wolff—Celtic peoples, who often sent their women into combat along with the men, simply referred to such an individual as a **Warrior Woman.** She is self-contained and thoroughly independent; she may act as a man's comrade or as his antagonist, but seldom as his sweet and dreamlike lover. She may function in the world of business as a contemporary career woman, or, if business annoys and bores her, she may find joy and personal fulfillment roaming free over the mountains and protecting the critters, a lover of wild nature like the Greek goddess Artemis. At her best, she is a high-minded seeker after her own path; at her worst, she is a steam-rolling dragon lady, insensitive to the needs of others and bent entirely upon her own personal self-aggrandizement.

Finally, there is the **Lover.** At one time in history, men thought of all women as either Mothers or Lovers. Nowadays, the Lover has fallen into disrepute among independent women, and she has been banished, like her patroness Aphrodite, to the backwaters of human history. Nevertheless, she remains alive and well within all women, and she must be reckoned with. She lives for others; she can find the light shining within a man and reveal to him his shadow, which she so longs to heal. She is ruled by her own individual feeling nature. Where the Queen thinks only in terms of one's role in society, the Lover ignores society altogether and is concerned only with the individual personality. As well as playing the role of a man's muse, she may also act as his sister or daughter. What she cannot do, sadly enough, is act like an independent adult. Afraid to commit, she wanders from one relationship to the next, seeking the warmth of a borrowed fire—but the older she gets, the more difficult it becomes to maintain her star-crossed course. At her best, she inspires others, especially men, to achieve their best—she is the love goddess, the muse, the sacred prostitute. She may also be something of an artist herself—a singer, dancer, or an actress. At her worst, she is an immature, clinging, and emotionally dependent slut. (Her polarities are a bit more extreme than those of the other types.)

At first glance, it may seem that these four primal roles or personalities are but variations on the eternal theme of the Triple Goddess, Maiden, Mother, and Crone. Do we not play the role of Warrior Woman or Lover during the Maiden phase of our lives? Do we not typically devote the middle years of life to the concerns of the Queen or Mother? Is not the Sorceress but

Figure 11: The Silver Wheel

another face of the Crone whose wisdom rules—or should rule—the latter years of a woman's existence?

To some degree, this is true. All women possess all four personality types within them, and as they progress along the road of the Silver Wheel, the different personalities may emerge more strongly to meet the demands of a changing life-path. Yet, in another sense, the four personality types are eternal rather than time-factored. A woman may be born a Lover, and, after marriage and child-bearing, she may struggle to learn the role of the Mother or Queen, to awaken that archetype within her. She may or may not be successful—after all, she was born a Lover and a Lover she will always remain.

We may think of the Silver Wheel as a wheel with four arms or spokes that remain fixed to their point of origin in the center; the center, however, turns round and round with the seasons of life.

Rhiannon has come forth from the womb of the unconscious and begun her road. She is the waxing moon, the Maiden in the first flush of her glory. As Maiden, she has two choices. She may spend this time alone, loving the wilderness and wild things, as did the Greek Artemis or the huntress Atalanta. In modern terms, she can become a tomboy, or, if she has a strong desire to expend her considerable energies in the outside world, she might become a Warrior Woman and go into business for herself.

Alternatively, she may enter into a relationship, embodying the archetype of the Lover. The fact that she pauses on her road to pay heed to Pwyll's wooing—indeed, she is, at least verbally, the instigator—tells us that she has chosen this second path, the path of relationship.

Before we follow her down that road, here is a test to help you determine which of the four primary female archetypes is most strongly embodied in you. Simply read the statements in each section of the test below and score according to how much or how little each statement applies to you. Circle the appropriate number indicated by the following numerical key:

3 = usually true
2 = moderately true
1 = rarely true
0 = almost never true

When you have completed the quiz, refer to the scoring columns at the end of the quiz to help you determine the mythic archetype that predominates in your life at this time.

One: The World at Large

A. I believe women must learn to achieve
   power and status in a man's world.   3   2   1   0

B. I am actively involved in social groups
   and community affairs.   3   2   1   0

C. I don't pay any attention to the daily news—
   I like to feel the world around me.   3   2   1   0

D. I am fascinated with everything under the sun;
   I love knowledge for the sake of knowledge. 3   2   1   0

Two: Reading Material

A. Politics, economics, and world history.   3   2   1   0

B. Psychology and New Age subjects.   3   2   1   0

C. Poetry, fiction, entertainment and the arts. 3   2   1   0

D. I'm too busy to read anything; I get my
   information from the televison.   3   2   1   0

Three: Friends

A. I prefer the company of those who
   can help my mate, my children, and myself
   to gain a better life.   3   2   1   0

B. I have spiritual or intellectual friendships. 3   2   1   0

C. Most of my friends are men.   3   2   1   0

D. My friends are my working colleagues.   3   2   1   0

Four: Social Events

A. I like to play the perfect hostess.   3   2   1   0

B. I'm uncomfortable at parties and often spend
   my time studying the other guests.   3   2   1   0

C. I just naturally present my most magnetic
side to everyone I meet.   3   2   1   0

D. I try to charm other people, and I am very
conscious of their enjoyment and welfare.   3   2   1   0

Five: Hobbies

A. I am always busy and have no time for hobbies.   3   2   1   0

B. Philosophy, religion, lectures.   3   2   1   0

C. Sports, exercise, animals.   3   2   1   0

D. Museums, art galleries, the theater.   3   2   1   0

Six: Children

A. I have no desire for children because
I am devoted to my inner path.   3   2   1   0

B. My children are an extension of myself.   3   2   1   0

C. I am fulfilled by my children; they are my
greatest achievements.   3   2   1   0

D. I love my children and care about
their emotional well-being.   3   2   1   0

Seven: Sex

A. Sex is essentially a mystical experience.   3   2   1   0

B. I flatter the maleness in traditional men.   3   2   1   0

C. Good sex is like a great session at the gym.   3   2   1   0

D. Sex is great, but romance is better.   3   2   1   0

Eight: Love and Commitment

A. A committed marriage enhances the safety
and well-being of my property.   3   2   1   0

B. Love and commitment require a higher
   spiritual dimension.   3   2   1   0

C. Love is all that matters.   3   2   1   0

D. A marriage commitment is
   important for one's social status.   3   2   1   0

Nine: Partners

A. I want a powerful partner who can equal
   my drive and energy.   3   2   1   0

B. I need a romantic, sexually exciting partner.   3   2   1   0

C. I need a partner who understands my need
   for both privacy and mental stimulation.   3   2   1   0

D. I need a partner who complements
   my position in the world.   3   2   1   0

Ten: Childhood

A. As a child, I loved to dream of knights, castles,
   and faraway lands.   3   2   1   0

B. As a child, I had imaginary playmates
   and created my own inner worlds.   3   2   1   0

C. I was the "den-mother" in all the childhood
   games I played with my friends.   3   2   1   0

D. As a child, I loved sports, critters,
   and the great outdoors.   3   2   1   0

Eleven: Food

A. I enjoy the atmosphere surrounding my meal
   as much as I enjoy the food itself.   3   2   1   0

B. I eat simply because it's necessary.   3   2   1   0

C. My table is a place of dignity and hospitality.   3   2   1   0

D. I am health-conscious and eat to stay fit.   3   2   1   0

Twelve: Residence

A. My home is my domain.   3   2   1   0

B. I like comfort and aesthetic surroundings.   3   2   1   0

C. My home is functional;
it is convenient to my work.   3   2   1   0

D. I need privacy and open spaces.   3   2   1   0

Thirteen: Physical Self

A. I pride myself on feeling active and fit.   3   2   1   0

B. I'm a very touchy-feely sort of person.   3   2   1   0

C. I am physically shy, sometimes embarrassed
by my body.   3   2   1   0

D. I often feel disconnected from my body.   3   2   1   0

Fourteen: Appearance

A. I dress for success.   3   2   1   0

B. I am a very fashionable girl.   3   2   1   0

C. I am conservative in my attire.   3   2   1   0

D. My appearance is rather offbeat and eccentric.   3   2   1   0

Scoring

On the scoring form below, list each of your answers for each question under the appropriate archetypal column. You will find the four letters, A–D, arranged under the female archetypes they represent.

Simply enter the number you circle for a particular statement next to its letter, like this:

Queen	Sorceress	Warrior Woman	Lover
1=B _2_	1=D _1_	1=A _3_	1=C _0_
2=D _1_	2=B _3_	2=A _2_	2=C _0_

Now add up the numbers for each female archetype column. The female archetypes that are strong within you will have the highest scores, and the weakest ones the low scores.

FEMALE ARCHETYPE SCORING COLUMNS

Queen	Sorceress	Warrior Woman	Lover
1=B ___	1=D ___	1=A ___	1=C ___
2=D ___	2=B ___	2=A ___	2=C ___
3=A ___	3=B ___	3=D ___	3=C ___
4=A ___	4=B ___	4=C ___	4=D ___
5=A ___	5=B ___	5=C ___	5=D ___
6=B ___	6=A ___	6=C ___	6=D ___
7=B ___	7=A ___	7=C ___	7=D ___
8=D ___	8=B ___	8=A ___	8=C ___
9=D ___	9=C ___	9=A ___	9=B ___
10=C ___	10=B ___	10=D ___	10=A ___
11=C ___	11=B ___	11=D ___	11=A ___
12=A ___	12=D ___	12=C ___	12=B ___
13=C ___	13=D ___	13=A ___	13=B ___
14=C ___	14=D ___	14=A ___	14=B ___
Totals: ___	___	___	___

Although this test was designed for women, men can also make use of it by answering each question in such a way as to describe the kind of women to whom they are attracted. Not only will this teach them a great deal about the kind of women they seek out for their relationships, but it will also tell them something about the nature of their own anima, the woman or "feminine side" within themselves.

Remember, we all see ourselves differently than others see us. If you feel really brave, get a friend to take the test as if she were describing you. You might be surprised to discover how different your own perceptions of yourself are from the perceptions of others around you.

Endnotes

1. Jeffrey Gantz, translator, *The Mabinogion* (London: Penguin, 1976), 51-55.

2. Sir James Frazer, *The Golden Bough* (New York: MacMillan Company, 1932), 207-210, 595-607.

3. Penelope Shuttle and Peter Redgrove, *The Wise Wound: The Myths, Realities, and Meanings of Menstruation* (New York: Grove Press, 1988), 27.

4. Ibid., 28.

5. Robert Graves, *The White Goddess* (New York: Farrar, Straus and Giroux, 1974), 384.

6. Ibid., 384-385.

7. Dr. Wolff wrote very little; a good résumé of her ideas can be found in Edward C. Whitmont, *The Symbolic Quest* (New York: Harper & Row, 1973), 178-184. The present authors have altered some of her concepts; for example, her original thesis postulated the Mother and Lover as one pair of opposites, the Amazon and Medium as another. We have chosen to follow a more Hermetic or magical schema based on the four seasons and the four elements, thus yielding two different pairs of opposites, i.e. Mother and Medium, Amazon and Lover.

8. See Robert Moore and Douglas Gillette, *King, Warrior, Magician, Lover: Rediscovering the Archetypes of the Mature Masculine* (San Francisco: Harper-SanFrancisco, 1990), and Kenneth Johnson and Marguerite Elsbeth, *The Grail Castle: Male Myths and Mysteries in the Celtic Tradition* (St. Paul, MN: Llewellyn Publications, 1995).

PART II

ALL HER
RELATIONS

CHAPTER TWO

The Magic Cup

We have all tasted various potions of love, and have found ourselves drunk with the magic of a new (and hopefully improved) romantic encounter. However, the sensation of being "in love" doesn't necessarily bring us the love we deserve....

By CHOOSING TO PAUSE upon her road and enter into a relationship with Pwyll, Rhiannon has chosen the same path that most women—at one time or another—will choose. As we have seen, a woman's *eros* endows her with a natural feeling of unity with all things, and hence it is part of her nature to relate. At some point in her life, she will take up the archetypal mask of the Lover.

Just because the path of relationship is a natural one for a woman to follow doesn't mean that it's easy. It is, in fact, a difficult way for anyone to take.

We live in a society based on romantic love. It is the subject of at least half our movies and television shows, as well as the root of a flourishing industry in "romance novels." It is part of our collective myth. For a teenage male to be "swept off his feet," to "fall in love"—and hence to act like a complete fool—is a virtual rite of passage in our world. Women are taught to groom themselves in order that they may become the worthy objects of such foolishness—the "popcorn Venus" of the media is damned close to being America's national female archetype. (This exalted position, occupied by Marilyn Monroe in the 1950s, is currently filled by Courtney Love, the "Goddess of Grunge." Others will follow, for we as a people can scarcely do without our Aphrodites.)

Venus herself must love, even as she is loved. Somewhere during the turbulent years of high school, she must learn to pine and sigh—whether for a football hero, academic miracle, or rebel with a peculiar haircut and vaguely defined artistic yearnings. Not only must she teach herself to sulk for love and remake herself in the image of the current reigning Aphrodite, but she must also learn to take it seriously. This, after all, is how we choose our partners for life! And why not? True love solves everything. Love makes the world go round.

Or does it?

Considering the form and function of relationships in Western society—we meet, fall in love, marry, become disillusioned, get divorced, and begin the process all over again—it is evident that our relationships are based on romantic idealism rather than the reality of love. Our brand of true love is comprised of a whole package of beliefs, attitudes, and expectations welling up from the depths of our souls. Thus we are often blindly dominated by our instinctual reactions and inherent primordial behavior patterns when seeking a potential life-mate.

The terminology of love is a dead giveaway. We "fall." We are "swept." We are "head over heels." All of this sounds more like a fatal plummet off a high cliff than the answer to all life's dilemmas.

What makes it all the more bewildering (at least from a mythological point of view) is that romantic love is a comparatively recent phenomenon. Our distant ancestors in Greece and Rome were seldom swept off their feet by the mad roller-coaster of love. Like present-day Chinese and Hindus, a marriage relationship in those days was based on stability, devotion, and loyalty to the cause of daily existence—common sense, if you will. Erotic love was something quite different, as well as being much less important— we may suspect that in those times, the archetype of the Lover and that of the Sacred Prostitute were one and the same. It was only in the Middle Ages that romantic love as we know it burst upon Western civilization like a

"If only there were a man," said Deirdre, "whose skin were as white as that snow, whose cheeks were as red as that blood, and whose hair was as black as those ravens!"

great spiritual flame. This event took place in France, especially the southern portion of that country, now called Provence. Medieval Provence was an unusual society, for women held the upper hand in many ways—thanks to the influence of powerful individuals like Eleanor of Aquitaine and her daughter Marie de Champagne. These women held festivals called "courts of love," where troubadour poets were invited to come and sing their poetry—poetry that was dedicated to the praise of the female principle. Our modern passion for romance first took shape in the context of such courts of love.

Yet this flowering of erotic love had been germinating underground for quite some time. Its roots may be discovered in the tales of the great, high-spirited lovers of Celtic mythology, our predecessors on the roller-coaster of love.

One of the oldest mythic cycles in Celtic lore is the so-called Ulster Cycle, a group of Irish tales and poems that chronicle the adventures of King Connor of Ulster and his band of warriors, the heroes of the Red Branch. Here, very early on, we find romantic love playing its exhilarating but disruptive role, for it was through the passionate love of a woman and a man that the Red Branch came to ruin.

Even before she was born, the woman called Deirdre was the subject of prophecy and foreboding: a soothsayer predicted that she would cause grief and destruction to countless men. It was nearly decided on to abandon the child on a heath, but when she was born she proved to be so beautiful that no one could think of harming her.

King Connor of Ulster took a personal interest in Deirdre. He found a nurse for her and had her sent away to a forest retreat—a "bothy" beneath the ground, a place so secret that it was often mistaken for a faery mound. Here Deirdre was raised, and grew to be the most beautiful woman in Ireland. No man was allowed to gaze upon her—none, that is, save King Connor himself, who regularly visited her and intended someday to marry her.

Then, one winter's day, a butcher slaughtered some bullocks not too far from Deirdre's forest hideaway. He left the blood in the snow. Deirdre and her nurse, walking in the wintry woods, saw the snow, the blood, and three black ravens picking at the blood.

"If only there were a man," said Deirdre, "whose skin were as white as that snow, whose cheeks were as red as that blood, and whose hair was as black as those ravens!"

The nurse told her that there was indeed such a man, and his name was Naoise. He was one of three brothers called the sons of Uisneach, and they were all members of the Red Branch.

From that moment on, Deirdre conspired to meet the man called Naoise. Her nurse, drawn into the plot, finally arranged for the two to meet in the forest. There they fell in love. Although Naoise was a member of the Red Branch, he abandoned his king and, aided by his two faithful brothers, carried Deirdre away.

They went to Scotland, where they lived in solitude for some years. At last, however, Fergus MacRoy, one of the champions of the Red Branch, came to find them. He told them that Connor was willing to forgive them and actually extended to them an invitation to a great feast. The brothers found the news welcome indeed, though Deirdre had dark forebodings. To quiet her suspicions, Fergus himself vouched for Connor's integrity, and swore that he and his sons would stand with the sons of Uisneach.

The four exiles returned to Ireland, but there was treachery in Connor's heart. For a taboo—called a *geis* in traditional Irish lore—had been laid upon Fergus that he must stop and drink whenever ale was offered. Connor made certain that tavern-keepers would offer Fergus plenty of ale on the road back to Ulster. So the sons of Uisneach arrived there without Fergus, who was drunk at some wayside inn. The brothers were housed in a house of thatch.

Connor sent one of his men to peek through the thatch and see if Deirdre was still as beautiful as ever—for if her glory had faded, then he would be willing to forgive the sons of Uisneach. The man was discovered peeping through the cracks and got his eye put out by Naoise, but he was able to report to Connor that Deirdre was still a marvel of beauty. Connor sent his men to attack the sons of Uisneach.

Thus was the great Ulster brotherhood broken, for the sons of Fergus stayed true to their father's wishes and fought alongside the sons of Uisneach against their Red Branch comrades. Many warriors died. The guest house was burned and the sons of Uisneach escaped with Deirdre into the forest. But their freedom lasted for only a little while—they were hunted down and the sons of Uisneach slain. Connor placed Deirdre in a chariot and began to drive her back to the palace. She never reached her destination alive—as the procession passed along a rocky mountain ridge, Deirdre flung herself out of the chariot and over the cliff.

The theme of romantic passion appears again in Irish legend, in a slightly later cycle of myths which centers on the character of Finn Mac-Cool. Finn was part warrior and part magician. He was the leader of a band of wilderness fighters called the Fiana. In his old age he became a widower, and went to the court of the High King Cormac mac Art at Tara, there to marry Cormac's daughter Grania.

During the wedding feast, Grania served the whiskey herself, going round and round till she had served everyone except the hero Dermot O'Dyna, son of the Gaelic love-god Angus mac Og. At that point she ran out of whiskey and went back to get some more, though when she returned to the hall everyone save Dermot was fast asleep—for indeed, the whiskey had been enchanted.

Fearing marriage to a man who was even older than her father, Grania begged Dermot to take her away. This Dermot was reluctant to do, for, after all, he was one of the Fiana and it was to Finn that he owed his loyalty. But in the end she prevailed upon him, and, sacrificing all, he ran off with her.

Dermot and Grania lived through many great adventures, for Finn and his warriors pursued them always, through a landscape rich with pure Celtic enchantment. Many times Dermot had to rely on his father, the love-god Angus, to spirit Grania away to safety while he stood his ground and fought against his former companions. But Dermot was the most accomplished warrior of them all, and always succeeded in getting away.

At last Finn grew weary of the pursuit and pardoned the two lovers. They lived happily enough for some time, until Grania became lonely and invited the two great men of Ireland, her father King Cormac and Finn himself, to come and visit them.

Dermot was lured away by the Fiana to fight with a wild boar atop a hill. Alas, there was a *geis* or taboo upon Dermot which forbade him to fight against boars, though he himself was unaware of the taboo. (Finn was perfectly aware of it, having heard about it from a Druid.) Dermot was badly wounded by the boar and called out for some water to sustain him. Finn went to gather water, but, remembering how Dermot had stolen Grania away, he allowed the water to drip out through his fingers, and so Dermot died.

But wait, you may say, are not these two stories fundamentally the same? In both cases a beautiful, headstrong young woman is to be married to a ruler somewhat older than herself, a man who is the chief of a great warrior brotherhood. Unable to tolerate marriage on such terms, the woman falls passionately in love with a young knight, a member of the brotherhood who must forsake his companions and fight against them for the sake of his lady-love. This in time brings tragedy to one and all.

Indeed, these two stories are one and the same. They may remind us of an even more famous story—one with which we are all very familiar.

King Arthur was, of course, the leader of the most famous brotherhood of all—the knights of the Round Table. He married Guinevere, and Guinevere fell madly in love with Lancelot, who, like Dermot O'Dyna, was the greatest warrior among a brotherhood of heroes. The love of Lancelot and Guinevere brought the Round Table to ruin.

This is, in fact, the one fundamental theme that runs as a common thread through the love-lore of the Celtic peoples. This story reached its greatest, most perfect form in the first (and perhaps still the best) love epic of Western civilization—the romance of Tristan and Iseult.[1]

Because Ireland had been imposing tribute on King Mark of Cornwall, the knight Tristan fought and killed the Morholt, the Irish champion. Tristan then journeyed to Ireland himself, to reap the rewards of his victory by obtaining the hand of Princess Iseult for King Mark. Iseult, the fierce and passionate daughter of a sorceress, loathed Tristan for slaying the Morholt, who by some accounts was her uncle, by others her fiancée. When Tristan first arrived in Ireland, Iseult wanted to kill him. On the sea journey back to Cornwall, however, something unusual happened.

According to a version of the legend recorded by Gottfried von Strassburg, Iseult's sorceress mother concocted a potion that would cause her daughter and King Mark to fall madly in love with each other. She entrusted the potion to Iseult's maid Brangaene, whom we shall call by the Celtic form of her name, Branwen. Two young maids in Iseult's entourage mistakenly served the potion to Tristan and Iseult during the homeward voyage, causing them to fall madly in love with each other.

An earlier version of the story by the French poet Beroul has been partially lost, including the scene in which Tristan and Iseult drink the magic drink. But it would seem that in this earlier tale, Branwen herself offered them the cup. This is most fitting from a mythic point of view, for Branwen was worshipped as a goddess of love in Pagan Cornwall. The cup was her magic implement; thus Tristan and Iseult drink the intoxicating nectar of the love goddess herself. Richard Wagner, in his opera *Tristan und Isolde,* presents two potions, one which causes love, the other, death. Iseult plots to kill both Tristan and herself with a poisoned cup. Her maid

Branwen, unwilling to see Iseult die, switches the poison and the love potion. Tristan and Iseult drink of the cup and fall in love.

Though Iseult is married to King Mark, her affair with Tristan continues. In time they are forced to run away together; Tristan deserts his king, just as Dermot deserted Finn and the sons of Uisneach abandoned Connor. Tristan and Iseult live deep within the forest (as did Dermot and Grania or Deirdre and Naoise), lost in the madness of love. Eventually, however, the lovers are reconciled with King Mark. Tristan goes over the sea to Brittany and marries another woman—who, interestingly enough, is also called Iseult. The new Iseult is no sorceress—rather, she represents the simplicity and practicality of daily life.

Daily life, however, holds no charms for Tristan. Gloomy and morose, he longs only for his sorceress—or, failing that, for death. Wounded in battle, he sends a trusted friend to seek out Iseult in Cornwall. If she will come to him, his friend will announce the fact by raising a white sail. If she refuses, let the sail be black.

Iseult hurries to her dying Tristan. But Tristan's wife, the other Iseult, is jealous. Seeing the white sail, she announces that it is black. And Tristan, too weak now to rise and see for himself, simply turns his head to the wall and dies. His wild Irish Iseult follows him in death, victim of "a broken heart."

Tristan and Iseult came to grief because they both sought perfection in each other rather than in themselves. But why do some women—and men, for that matter—get caught in this age-old trap?

What we call "romance" is all too often a simple case of psychological projection. From a mystical standpoint, each of us is androgynous, for each of us, woman and man alike, contains the totality of the universe—fire and water, yin and yang, male and female. Within each woman lies a silent, unconscious "other half," her male self, which Jung called the animus. Similarly, every man contains an "inner woman," his muse or anima. As we walk the path of life, we all seek our universal totality, our spiritual completeness. But we all too often seek it in the wrong places.

When a woman falls in love with a man—especially when she is "swept off her feet" or experiences "love at first sight"—she has actually fallen in love with herself! Only a spiritual entity, something numinous and shining, is genuinely capable of making her feel as if she's tasted the divine nectar in Branwen's cup. Men, on the other hand, are ordinary mortals, and ordinary mortals are simply that—ordinary and mortal. So what a woman really sees when she gazes into her beloved's eyes is her own animus.

In many cases, a woman's animus is not exactly a pure spiritual being. He may be so potentially—and in time he may become her inner torch-bearer, leading her to an understanding of the *logos* aspect of consciousness—but in the beginning he is likely to carry on his back all the unconscious garbage and detritus stored within her own primal brain.

This, of course, makes him less like a god and more like the Demon Lover, a figure that appears in many old Celtic ballads. The men a woman chooses under such unconscious auspices are likely to turn into demons themselves—her own personal demons, to be precise.

Thus we seek our own completeness and perfection through our relationships. The object of our love and devotion becomes a mirror image of the qualities we would most like to see in ourselves. For some reason, however, we fear that we lack these qualities, or else we don't really want to work hard enough to develop these traits. Then the mirror image shifts to show its opposite face—all our own weaknesses, frailties, and negative habits appear there. When we see our own image reflected in the mirror of another, all kinds of things can happen.

This is why a woman's animus, the man within her, seldom waltzes into her dreams (or her waking life) decked out like Prince Charming, his protective sword in one hand and a lover's rose in the other. More often than not, dreams and fairytales show him first as a strange, dark force, perhaps invisible. He is the sense of dread or threat lingering on the boundaries of a dream. He is the black stallion whose appearance bodes change and transformation. He is the sorcerer, come to lock you in the tower. In the dreams of modern women, he may also appear as the terrorist who holds you hostage at a bank, the serial killer who stalks you through a nightmare.

Yet this dark pursuer, this Demon Lover who embodies everything disturbing and demented in the collective psyche of men everywhere, is the animus in disguise. Like Psyche in the Greek myth, you may fear that he is a beast, but when you approach him in the dark and study his face in the light of a lamp—which is nothing less than his own torch of *logos*—you will see that he is beautiful, a god. Then, like Theseus in yet another Greek myth, he will unravel the thread of your soul, travel into the darkness of your labyrinth (once again bearing his torch), and kill the minotaur who lives there.

As we have seen, all human beings are androgynous. We all partake equally of *eros* and *logos*. A man, if he is fortunate, will find his *eros* or his anima through music or poetry, rather than dumping her in your lap (you have better things to do). A woman may seek her *logos* in a healthy way by seeking her inner creative fires, gaining empowerment and independence, and thus lighting the torch the animus bears.

In a sense, these old Celtic tales speak with a contemporary voice, for Deirdre, Grania, and Iseult are curiously modern—they flaunt tradition and seek the self, even if they mistakenly seek it in a partner. All of them are notable for their strong will. These women are never weak and needy. Rather, they are fully empowered. Deirdre commands Naoise and his kin to carry her away, and Grania places an entire hall of revelers under a spell in order to force Dermot to spirit her off. Iseult, too, has sorceress blood in her veins. One suspects that all of them, proudly scoffing at tradition, would have been happier without mates. Wild women, after all, are always happier running free, playing the role of Warrior Woman or Amazon, with critters following in their wake while they listen to the voices of the trees. We may well ask ourselves why they need relationships in the first place!

When a woman has found her own animus and is operating from a non-traditional standpoint, roaming the woods in heady isolation (or deriving pleasure from drag-racing as opposed to getting her hair done), she is certain to be perceived as "masculine" in nature. In reality, however, she is simply manifesting dynamic, assertive, passionate, free, and self-realized behavior. The Lover may be primarily a young woman's archetype, but so is its opposite, the Warrior Woman—and all things contain their opposites, as the world's great mystical traditions have affirmed for thousands of years. In such cases, a woman's eternal child, her I AM, has come out to play, displaying courage and energy along with a certain naivete. The dark side of this self-empowerment leads to impulsive and selfish actions, as well as manipulation, domination, and control. Sadly, this comes from the fact that such a woman may not be readily accepted by others, or even by herself. Therefore she can appear as the suspicious antagonist or odd loner who doesn't seem to care about people. She may also be "the entitled one" who seeks preferential treatment, as well as the compulsive character who expects nothing short of perfection. Similarly, this energy may be demonstrated through power, solitude, self-improvement, and decisiveness.

Our Celtic lovers have chosen the path of relationship rather than solitude, the Lover as opposed to the Warrior Woman. They have erred, as many modern women err, in seeking the empowerment of the animus through a lover's eyes. The empowerment that women gain in this fashion won't last long, for a man will run away from the responsibility of playing your Sir Lancelot and bearing your torch, just as surely as you will run away from the onus of acting out his inner "popcorn Venus," washing the dishes while clad only in a garter belt.

A woman who has not yet made her peace with the torch-bearer within is likely to have the kind of relationship problems experienced by our trio of Celtic lovers. Such a woman is, in fact, dominated by the animus. Jungian analysts speak of such a woman as being "animus-ridden," for her violent struggles with the man within have resulted in his temporary ascendancy. There may be themes involving intimidation, abuse, detachment, and self-righteousness. All of these temperamental traits may describe a woman whose path along the Silver Wheel has become a giddy and tempestuous tightrope. Madly in love with her own animus, she fiercely rejects traditional viewpoints and behaviors. But she is still young, and the animus is yet a mystery, a creature not yet fully known and hence capable of striking out with wild and inexplicable frenzy, with what Shakespeare might have called "an antic disposition"—a disposition that frightens the woman herself as much as those around her.

We have all tasted various potions of love, and have found ourselves drunk with the magic of a new (and hopefully improved) romantic encounter. However, the sensation of being "in love" doesn't necessarily bring us the love we deserve, nor does it protect us from the fatal flaws that some relationships carry within them. Many of us fall prey to deadly love myths which compel us to believe the false notions we may have regarding ourselves or others. When we find ourselves believing that "true love conquers all," that "love at first sight" will last forever, that powerful sexual chemistry equals love, or that there is only one true love in the world for us and that that person will fulfill us in every way, then we are preventing ourselves from making intelligent love choices. When a difficult relationship pattern is involved, it can lead us into sexually addictive, abusive, or obsessive relationships. Whether we act on unconscious desires or preconceived notions of what love is suppposed to be, the assertive and empowered woman who has emerged from the faery mound into an intense consciousness of self may manifest her urge to possess the lover in many ways.

A woman may become antagonistic by manipulating herself to be suspicious, solitary, oppositional, and intimidating, and by manipulating others to act as if they are dependent and afraid. An antagonist believes that she needs to be vigilant; she needs to "get" others before she herself is "had." Therefore her manipulative strategy includes wariness and the subtle techniques of the interrogator, including isolating the loved one from the things he loves best. Dermot, Tristan, and the sons of Uisneach were all forced to forsake their companions and remove themselves to the wilderness to hold on to the powerful and assertive women they loved.

Sometimes a woman is detached from the world at large, and may cast herself in the role of the eccentric, self-sufficient loner who doesn't particularly care about others. She may therefore pattern others to become distant, disinterested, or disparaging in their behavior. Loners believe that relationships are messy, irritable things, definitely not worth the trouble; people are somehow irrelevant. Their controlling strategy includes staying away, remaining aloof, and not needing or caring for anyone. Deirdre was raised in an isolated barrow in the woods, and had a loner's typical disdain for others. She felt no qualms about commanding Naoise—and his two innocent brothers—to surrender their lives to her whim. Throughout her story, she remains an aloof and lofty character, who only touches us now and again through her sense of tragic grandeur.

Some women have a tendency to feel more entitled than others— again like Deirdre, or for that matter, like Grania, who felt entitled to place all of Finn's men under a spell and run off with the one she desired, simply because she desired it. Such women may sometimes deceive themselves through narcissistic and superior behavior, seeking preferential treatment through social status and powerful positions. In this way, they mislead others to be subservient followers, even as Dermot and Naoise followed the wishes of Grania and Deirdre in all things. Entitled types believe they are better than others. They are heroines who should be ardently worshipped by all. Their idea of "good management" may include boasting as a means to mesmerize others with their own grandiosity.

Compensating for society's lack of acceptance of non-traditional mores, an assertive woman may become downright aggressive—especially when her inner sorceress or wild woman runs the show, as Iseult's mother "ran" things from behind the scenes with Branwen's help. Thus a woman may become obsessive, compulsive, perfectionistic, self-righteous, and— paradoxically—somewhat indecisive at the same time. This induces others to act fawning and obsequious, seeking her approval. Obsessive-compulsive types (all three of the lovers we have examined are certainly that) like to uphold standards of perfection in all things. They moralize, lecture, and criticize, and are impatient with the weaknesses and frailties inherent in human nature (especially their own).

What does this all mean? Is such a woman, as she sometimes seems to be, a wild sex fiend demanding abject worship and subservience from others? Is she a man-hating Amazon who should be banished to the outlands for not having her nails honed and polished every week?

The difference between Tristan—a man gentle enough to win accolades in today's New Age community—and his wild love is this: Tristan falls victim to "the other" because he fails to recognize the self, whereas Iseult preys upon the other because all she can recognize is the numinous glow of her masculine self.

How, then, shall a woman maintain the delicate balance necessary in relationships without at the same time losing command of herself?

She must transform the Demon Lover into a prince. This is the internal metamorphosis that sweeps the soul in a process of alchemical transmutation. If she fails, a woman may become animus-ridden, like Iseult, Deirdre, or Grania. But how is such a task accomplished?

Let us return to the story of Rhiannon.[2] As you might remember, we left her on the road, having made a tryst with Pwyll, Prince of Dyved. In a year's time, he was to put in an appearance at the court of Rhiannon's father, Heveydd the Old, to claim her from the confines of a marriage to which she objected.

After a year passed, Pwyll traveled with ninety-nine riders to the court of Heveydd the Old. Rhiannon was anxiously waiting for him.

Following meat, a red-headed youth of royal demeanor entered the hall, greeted Pwyll and his companions, and asked him for a favor. Pwyll's response was somewhat grandiose:

"Ask for whatever you want, and I shall give it to you."

Aghast, Rhiannon turned to Pwyll and said, "Why have you given such an answer?"

But Pwyll kept on. "Friend, what is it you want?"

The youth replied, "I ask that tonight I may sleep with the lady I love best, and I come here to ask for her."

Pwyll was dumbstruck by the youth's bold reply. Rhiannon said angrily, "Be silent as long as you wish, for never was there a man more witless than you!"

Pwyll tried to make excuses, but Rhiannon continued, "That is Gwawl, son of Clud, whom I do not wish to marry, despite his wealth. Now you must give me to him because you have given your word."

"I can't do it," said Pwyll.

"Do it," whispered Rhiannon, "and I shall fix it so that he shall never have me."

A deal was made: in a year's time, Gwawl would return to the court of Heveydd the Old and possess Rhiannon. And return he did. A great feast was provided for him, but while he was making merry with Rhiannon by his side, Pwyll was outside in the garden with his ninety-nine men. Dressed like a beggar, he entered the hall, and asked a boon of Gwawl.

"All I want is to fill my little bag with food," he said.

That sounded simple enough, and Gwawl set his servants to doing just that. But Pwyll's little bag was a magic one, and it was bottomless. The entire feast began to disappear into it.

"How can we finish this?" asked Gwawl.

"A great lord must stomp down the food already in the bag," replied Pwyll.

"You're my champion," Rhiannon told Gwawl. "You do the stomping."

Gwawl leapt onto the bag with his big boots and began to stomp. Pwyll quickly turned the bag upside down and pulled the drawstring tight, capturing Gwawl in the bag. Then came each of the ninety-nine men, all of whom whacked at the bag till Gwawl begged for mercy and ran off with his tail between his legs.

And thus Pwyll won Rhiannon after all.

Gwawl's role in the story is a curious one. Rich and red-headed, he bursts onto the scene to seize the woman of his dreams. Rhiannon, of course, has no wish to be seized—this is more like an abduction, a kidnapping of the soul. Is Gwawl the Demon Lover? His name is revealing. Gwawl, son of Clud means "Wall, son of Clyde." There was, in Celtic and medieval times, a wall along the river Clyde, separating Roman Britain from the wild blue-painted Picts who lived to the north. Gwawl, then, represents the savage darkness on the other side of the wall.

Rhiannon tricked Gwawl, and thereby found the husband of her desire. But she made one mistake—one that will haunt her later on.

You can't trick the Demon Lover. You can't hit him with a stick and make him go away.

We can find a splendid example of this problem in men's mythology. As he is engaged in his quest, Perceval the Grail Knight constantly encounters an antagonist called the Red Knight. He fights the Red Knight, defeats and kills him—then finds him waiting round the bend at the start of his next adventure! It is only when Perceval recognizes the Red Knight as one of his own relatives and shakes hands with him that he can finally stop fighting.

It is only when a woman recognizes the Demon Lover as a portion of herself and makes friends with him that he turns into a prince. Sticking him in a bag and beating him just won't help.

Perhaps the most powerful story of a woman's struggle with the Demon Lover in all of Celtic lore is the folk ballad titled "Tam Lin."[3] No one knows exactly when and where this Scottish song had its origins, but it was already old in 1549 and is thoroughly Pagan in spirit.

> *O I forbid you maidens all,*
> *That wear gold on your hair,*
> *To come or go by Carterhaugh*
> *For young Tam Lin is there.*

There's none that goes by Carterhaugh
But they leave him a pledge,
Either their rings, or green mantles,
Or else their maidenhead.

Janet has kilted her green kirtle
A little above her knee,
And she has braided her yellow hair
A little above her bree, *
And she's away to Carterhaugh,
As fast as she can hie.

We may admire Janet's spunk, but the girl is clearly looking for trouble. The place called Carterhaugh is haunted by a Demon Lover called Tam Lin, and a woman who answers the call of unconscious compulsion by seeking him out can expect to return sadder and wiser. Janet, however, jumps at the chance. She has heard the cry of the Beast stirring within her, and all she can do is hike up her skirts and run like an Olympic track star, straight into the arms of her own dark-spirited animus.

She had not pulled a double rose,
A rose but only two,
Till up then started young Tam Lin,
Says, "Lady, thou's pull no more."

In Scottish lore, certain magical plots of earth are called "faery gardens," for it is here that the "good folk" reside, just beyond the realm of our own senses, in a barrow mound below. The lord of a faery garden can be summoned by pulling on a nut tree, sloeberry, or, in this case, a "double rose." Tam Lin emerges from beneath the earth; he is elvish.

Who, then, are the elves, the faery people? Some writers, like the late Margaret Murray,[4] believed them to be the surviving members of an older race that inhabited the British Isles during Neolithic times (6000–1800 B.C.). Others have deemed them nature spirits of one type or another. In

---

* Brow.

Ireland, the faery folk are the *sidhe*, and the *sidhe* are none other than the old Pagan goddesses and gods. Banished from the world by the force of Christianity, they persist below the earth, living in the great barrow mounds that dot the Irish landscape.

It was from such a barrow mound that Rhiannon emerged, was it not? Whether the elves and faery folk represent the spirits of our most ancient ancestors, the forces of nature, or the "old gods," they are clearly archetypal forces, dwelling in the collective unconscious for which the barrow mound is but a symbol.

The Demon Lover has emerged from Janet's unconscious. How shall they relate with one another?

"Why pull'st thou the rose, Janet,
And why breaks thou the wand?
Or why comes thou to Carterhaugh
Withouten my command?"

"Carterhaugh, it is my own,
My daddy gave it me;
I'll come and go by Carterhaugh,
And ask no leave of thee."

As we have seen, the Demon Lover usually makes his first appearance in a woman's dreams—or waking life—as a threatening figure, full of menace. Tam Lin behaves in similar fashion. But Janet, an admirable girl indeed, isn't having that. She argues with him.

You can't fight the shadow, now can you? Rhiannon can't put Gwawl in a bag and beat him till he goes away.

Poor Janet....

He's ta'en her by the milk-white hand
Below the grass-green sleeve,
And he's laid her low at the foot of a wand
And never once asked her leave.

She turned her right and round about
To ask her true love's name;
But she nothing heard, and she nothing saw,
But all the woods grew dim.

When a woman resists the arrival of the animus, he is certain to try and take over by force. Tam Lin has "ridden" Janet in fine fashion, taken possession without even "asking her leave."

A woman may experience the dark animus psychologically, as when she becomes possessed by rage, by great passions of irrationality (which, to her, seem to be perfectly logical), or even when she suddenly becomes determined to take control in a man's world and steamroll her way through a major corporation. She may also experience him through projection, attracting a dark, treacherous, perhaps even dangerous man into her life. Either way, she will awaken from the spell alone, wondering, left with the echo of magic in her soul and aching with the passion of an archetypal encounter that may have been agonizing, ecstatic, or both.

Yet the encounter has not left Janet unscarred, as she discovers when she returns to her father's hall.

Out then spoke her father dear,
And he spoke meek and mild,
"And ever alas, sweet Janet," he says,
"I think you go with child."

"If I go with child, father,
Myself must bear the blame;
There's ne'er a laird about your hall
Shall get the bairn's name.

"If my lover were an earthly knight,
As he's an elfin grey,
I would not give my own true-love
For nae lord that ye hae."

A seed has been planted within. Even though he has appeared in his shadow form, the animus has nevertheless lighted the inner torch, and now Janet cannot turn back from seeking her own individuality. The embryo of a more complete self, sharpened with the tough individual edge of the *logos*, is growing like a child in her womb.

But how can she trust the darkness? How can a mortal woman couple with an "elfin grey" and still walk upon solid ground? Janet hurries back to the faery garden at Carterhaugh and pulls on the rose again. She demands a bit of history from Tam Lin.

"Roxbrugh he was my grandfather,
Took me with him to bide,
And once it fell upon a day
That woe did me betide.

"And once it fell upon a day,
A cold day and a snell, *
When we were from the hunting come,
That from my horse I fell;
The Queen of Faerys she caught me,
In yon green hill to dwell.

"And pleasant is the faery land,
But, an eerie tale to tell,
Aye at the end of seven years
We pay a tithe to hell;
I am so fair and full of flesh,
I'm feared it be myself.

"But the night is Halloween, lady,
The morn is Hallowday;
Then win me, win me, and ye will,
For well I wat ye may.

* Gloomy and damp.

"Just at the mirk and midnight hour
The faery folk will ride,
And they that would their true-love win,
At Miles Cross they must bide."

Tam Lin dwells in the great barrow mound of the unconscious, and, as the shadowy side of Janet's male self, he is in great danger of descending even farther down, into a darkness so deep that she will never be able to reclaim him. A woman's animus may easily sink into the ultimate depths—manifesting as a rapist, stalker, psychopath—and never complete the transformation into the godlike bearer of the torch of consciousness.

If she wants to transform Tam Lin, Janet must fight for him. The hosting of the faery folk described in the song is a familiar theme in Celtic myth; it also goes by the name of the Wild Hunt. Led by an Otherworldy king or queen, all the ghosts of the departed, all the spirits of the Otherworld, race through the midnight in a dark, shadowy mass. The Wild Hunt was an apparition frequently seen during medieval times, and one that terrified the ordinary peasant (the brave souls who gladly joined in the Wild Hunt were usually executed as witches). This is the terror that Janet must face. As Tam Lin instructs her, she must wait at Miles Cross, behold the terrifying Wild Hunt, and find Tam Lin. She must pull him down from his horse. In other words, she must learn to find her own *logos* among the myriad shifting forms and illusions of the unconscious mind.

Suppose she succeeds. What then? Has she won the game?

No, not yet. Not by any means.

"They'll turn me in your arms, lady,
Into an esk* and adder;
But hold me fast, and fear me not,
I am your bairn's father.

"They'll turn me to a bear so grim,
And then a lion bold;
But hold me fast, and fear me not,
As ye shall love your child.

---

* A lizard.

"Again they'll turn me in your arms
To a red hot gaud of iron;
But hold me fast, and fear me not,
I'll do to you no harm.

"And last they'll turn me in your arms
Into the burning gleed; *
Then throw me into well water,
O throw me in with speed."

The ability of the animus to take on new and frightening forms is almost limitless. That elvish strain within us all—that which dances in the moonlight, which remembers ancient magics—is a shapeshifter of great power. The more a woman tries to transform the animus, the more he will twist and turn. He will take on the shape of each and every one of her unconscious fears, demons, and desires. Such a woman may find herself possessed by rage or the will to dominate again and again, no matter how hard she tries to control it. Such a woman may find herself vowing, over and over, never to involve herself with a particular kind of jerk—only to discover that her next candidate for Mr. Right sooner or later removes his mask to reveal the same familiar demon underneath.

There is no panacea to lead a woman through the labyrinth, but there is a solution. She needs courage and faith. She has to hold on to the image within. In time it will become her own image, the power of her own *logos* seen as an inner force, an empowering force, and stripped of all its illusory disguises.

"And then I'll be your own true-love,
I'll turn a naked knight;
Then cover me with your green mantle,
And cover me out of sight."

Janet makes the journey to Miles Cross, and holds tightly to Tam Lin through all his transformations. Now she can see him as he really is—a naked

---

* A glowing coal.

knight. Thus any woman can learn to see men as they really are—as human beings rather than archetypal figures. Then she becomes capable of having an actual relationship with a real person. And the animus? Covered with a mantle of green, he disappears back inside her, for she has recognized him as a part of herself. Janet has succeeded by reconciling two of the great opposites of the female path: she is Lover and Warrior Woman at one and the same time.

Naturally assertive women, should they desire to enter into a relationship, must eventually learn to recognize that intimate love relationships are a way to care for, honor, and celebrate the partner on a daily basis, as an expression of commitment to one another. As with all contacts between a woman's "inner man" and a man's "inner woman" (the animus and anima of Jungian psychology), when they feel impelled to love another they are actually seeking a road that will enable them to love themselves. Real commitment occurs in the heart, and is ultimately reflected in the way we (men and women alike) treat our mates. A woman is ready for commitment when she has freed Tam Lin by working through whatever obstacles or emotional issues are hindering growth. Women who find it difficult to respond to men in a constructive way need to develop faith and trust in their relationships and in their ability to continue to grow and survive adversity. Women must overcome their reticence to act, and learn to feel excited about exploring the subterranean levels of love, intimacy, and surrender.

This anonymous folk song—probably handed down by generations of women, since its psychology is essentially feminine—provides us with one model for capturing the Demon Lover and making him real. There are others, as we shall see later on in these pages, when Rhiannon comes to face the consequences of trying to shove Gwawl into a bag and hide him away. In fact, the game of love, terror, and pursuit that women play with their Demon Lovers leads them spiraling down to the ultimate depths of transformation and the ultimate peaks of transcendence. It is a game that is never altogether finished.

Human beings are naturally tribal creatures, meant to live in group situations. Life can never be free of relationships, because relationships are everything. We share a relationship with our mail carrier because she or he delivers and we pick up. Eating requires that we have an intimate relationship with plants and animals. We have a direct relationship with the weather, for it determines the quality of our existence. We are all one people. Our goal is to live in unity and harmony with all of life. Willing acceptance, loving kindness, and a little human sympathy really can make bad feelings go away. We all need to be valued and noticed for our individual worth in order to develop further self-confidence. Creating a good, healthy relationship is like cooking a delicious meal. It requires the right mixture of ingredients, foremost of which are faith, hope, and love.

The test that follows measures your relationship with the animus. Has he been projected onto another? Are you "ridden" by him like a horse? Or does he carry his torch in bright internal splendor while the conscious, total you is in outer control?

	YES	NO
1. Do you think you have a dynamic personality?	_____	_____
2. Are you passionate and assertive when expressing your feelings?	_____	_____
3. Are you naive and childlike in your expectations?	_____	_____
4. Are you courageous in the face of danger?	_____	_____
5. Do you feel that you can overcome any obstacle by sheer force of will?	_____	_____
6. Are you impulsive and foolhardy when entering into an intimate relationship?	_____	_____
7. Do you tend to be selfish or have a "me-first" attitude?	_____	_____
8. Do you believe the romantic notion that your partner wants to be told what to do?	_____	_____
9. Is it "my way or the highway" if your partner doesn't comply with your wishes?	_____	_____
10. Do you become combative and argumentative at the slightest provocation?	_____	_____
11. Do you have a double standard, or offer your partner choices without really meaning it?	_____	_____
12. Are you reticent to act on your own behalf or on the behalf of others?	_____	_____
13. Are you antagonistic when others disagree with you?	_____	_____
14. Do you believe you are entitled to preferential treatment?	_____	_____

	YES	NO

15. Are you an isolationist who likes to be alone?

16. Do you seek out rejection in the form of unavailable partners or partners who reinforce your own negative patterns?

17. Are you "the wise one" in your relationships?

18. Are you unconscious about the things you do or say?

19. Do you feel extreme jealousy, ambivalence, or guilt which sometimes results in abusive actions toward yourself or others?

20. Do you have a compulsive need to "stir things up" when a relationship is going well?

Scoring

Questions 1 through 5 represent the positive side of the Amazon or Warrior Woman, she who has entered into a genuine and fulfilling inner relationship with her animus. A majority of *yes* answers in this area indicates a healthy use of assertive energy. A majority of *no* answers suggests that you need to work on issues requiring self-assertion.

Questions 6 through 15 indicate a conflict with self-assertiveness. A majority of *yes* answers in this section means that there is work for you to do in the area of passion vs. compassion. A majority of *no* answers indicates a strong self-identity coupled with the ability to empathize with others.

Questions 16 through 20 indicate even deeper problems with self-assertion. A majority of *yes* answers in this section indicates the need for self-confidence as well as self-control, while a majority of *no* answers suggests sensitivity and tolerance when interacting with others.

Endnotes

1. Joseph Bedier, translated by Hilaire Belloc and Paul Rosenfeld, *The Romance of Tristan and Iseult* (New York: Vintage Books, 1945).

2. Gantz, *The Mabinogion*, 55-58.

3. This version is based on the one in MacEdward Leach, editor, *The Ballad Book* (New York: A. S. Barnes and Company, 1975), 136-141. The Scottish dialect has been edited into a more contemporary idiom.

4. See *The Witch Cult in Western Europe* (London: Oxford University Press, 1921), and *The God of the Witches* (London: Oxford University Press, 1970).

CHAPTER THREE

The Starling and the Owl

Changing old systems of belief and patterns of behavior takes time. One phase of the process of awakening, of entering into womanhood, is recognizing those moments when the wind of a higher power—the wind of the Otherworld—is blowing through our lives, seeking to move us to a new place, a new level of awareness....

I<small>N ORDER TO SUCCEED</small> in the heady ring-dance of relationships, we must be able to merge the opposites of existence. Even when women attempt to embody their *eros* and merge with another, they must still employ a bit of *logos* and learn to discriminate—to know which relationships, or kinds of relationships, will be healthy for them. This is the role of the animus, whose torchlight shines in the dark places and teaches women to perceive with clarity. This is the gift for which Janet wrestled Tam Lin with such courage and passion.

The truth, however, is that most of us—women and men alike—still have trouble making such decisions or reaching such conclusions. After all, life has many variables, and we want the end result to be perfect. We experience distress at the thought of detaching ourselves from the result of our desire. Knowing what we want in a partner, in a friend, out of life, inevitably begins with self-knowledge, a willingness to be oneself. To make a relationship work, a readiness to compromise part of oneself for the sake of another must exist. We must be willing to let go.

Sometimes, however, we let go of too much. One may admire Iseult, Deirdre or Janet for their headstrong willpower, the fire and passion with which they express themselves. Many women will admire them precisely because they feel that they themselves lack these qualities—for if half the women in contemporary society feel a new and vital sense of empowerment, the other half still feel locked in a dark prison of passivity.

The second tale in the *Mabinogion* is titled "Branwen, Daughter of Llyr."[1] Though Branwen is depicted in this story simply as a princess, sister of King Bran, it is clear that she was once an aspect of the Goddess, for, as we have seen, she was once worshipped as the goddess of love in Cornwall; her primary attribute was a cup, which is certainly the "loving cup" of medieval legend. Though she bears the title of Queen, she is in fact the archetypal Lover.

Branwen's story proves to be a sad one. According to the *Mabinogion*, she was the most beautiful woman in the world. Her brother, King Bran, gave her in marriage to Mallolwch, King of Ireland. But the marriage was soured almost before it began. Branwen's half-brother Evnissyen, angry because no one had consulted him concerning the upcoming marriage, mutilated King Mallolwch's horses. This, of course, was a dreadful insult to the Irish. Bran tried to make amends by giving Mallolwch more horses, as well as a great and magical gift: a cauldron into which dead warriors could be tossed to be reborn.

Despite these gifts, the King of Ireland continued to brood. Branwen bore him a son called Gwern, but even this failed to provide any warmth to the marriage. In time, Branwen was reduced to laboring as a kitchen maid, scrubbing pots like Cinderella. All trade and communication between Ireland and Wales was forbidden, to prevent King Bran from learning of his sister's sorry fate.

But Branwen found a baby starling by the kitchen, and raised it to become her creature. She fastened a message to the bird, telling of her plight, and sent it flying back to Wales. In time her brother Bran came to her rescue. So mighty was he that no house could hold him. Therefore Mallolwch had the notion of placating Bran by building a house of gigantic size for him—as well as giving up the monarchy to Gwern, son of Branwen.

She begged him to stay and become her husband—or even her illicit lover—but Lancelot gently explained that he was devoted to the queen....

Bran accepted the proposal, but Mallolwch still intended to trick him, hiding warriors in the new house. Wild Evnissyen, who had caused all the trouble by mutilating Mallolwch's horses, discovered the plot and foiled it—but then turned around and caused more trouble. Just as the new king, young Gwern, was being presented to the assemblage, Evnissyen grabbed the boy and threw him into the hearth-fire.

A great commotion ensued, followed by a battle between the Irish and the Welsh. The Irish were winning—after all, they had the Cauldron of Rebirth, and their warriors were restored to life as soon as they had been killed. Evnissyen at last redeemed himself by leaping into the cauldron and "stretching himself out" until both he and the cauldron burst.

The Welsh prevailed, but at great cost. Bran himself was mortally wounded with a magical wound. Gwern was dead. When Branwen finally arrived once more on the coast of Wales, she lay down and died of a broken heart.

She wasn't the only one. A most tragic Arthurian tale, very popular in Queen Victoria's day, concerns Elaine, the Lily Maid of Astolat (or Shalott, in Alfred Lord Tennyson's syrupy Victorian poem). One day Sir Lancelot, traveling in disguise, stopped at the castle of Astolat. The lord of the castle entertained him well, and the lord's daughter, Elaine, was smitten with the stranger. Lancelot, still in disguise, traveled with Elaine's brother to a great tournament. He fought with and conquered all the knights of King Arthur's court, who failed to recognize him because he wore on his helmet the standard or "favor" of the Lily Maid of Astolat—whereas everyone knew that the great Sir Lancelot never wore the favor of any lady save Queen Guinevere. Wounded in the jousting, Lancelot returned to Astolat with his companion, who placed the wounded hero under the tender care of his sister Elaine—who, after all, was mad for Lancelot in the first place.

Elaine healed the stranger, who lingered in Astolat. Eventually a group of Arthur's knights passed by the castle and recognized their old companion. The lord of the castle and his son realized just whom they'd been entertaining for so long—and so did Elaine. She begged him to stay and become her husband—or even her illicit lover—but Lancelot gently explained that he was devoted to the queen, and he left.

Elaine's response was somewhat unbalanced, to say the least. She allowed herself to pine away even unto death, then placed herself on a magnificent barge which began to float (on its own, of course, for everything was magical in those days) to Camelot. There she was discovered by King Arthur's court—lying on her bier, golden-haired, beautiful, and dead. In her little purse was a note explaining that it was all Lancelot's fault.

Or was it? Perhaps it was Elaine's own fault, for not having the courage to make a life for herself that was independent of her relationships.

In the last chapter, we met a trio of fierce women who sought the self courageously, though they made the desperate mistake of seeking it in the eyes of another. Branwen and Elaine, however, seem to have abandoned the self entirely. In this respect, they too are our contemporaries. For if many modern women fearlessly seek the self, there are an equal number who keep trying to relinquish it. This, of course, is the Lover's eternal dilemma; she lives only through her relationships.

Like many contemporary women, Branwen exists solely as wife and mother—given away in a political marriage and condemned to a life of drudgery. Finally, she calls out for help; she sends one sad starling into the sky. Her cry for help brings disaster; most of the men in the story die (her husband Mallolwch, her brothers Bran and Evnissyen, and her son Gwern). Then, without a relationship to sustain her, all she can do is lie down and join them. Elaine of Astolat was equally dependent on her relationship with Lancelot.

Many women who, through choice or natural disposition, take up the mask of Aphrodite and play the Lover's role in life have been in Branwen's or Elaine's position—their relationships have left them with no life, no vision, seemingly no soul of their own. This, clearly, is not the goal of relationships, but it is all too common in our own age and society. Sooner or later, the first glowing and glorious feelings of "falling" in love will pass, and some very sobering realities will remain. Like Branwen, the contemporary Lover is banished to the grubby kitchen work of the heart, with only a bird—universal symbol of the soul—for company.

It was at this point that Branwen's soul cried out, took flight, sought release. But not all women behave like goddesses all the time. Sometimes they stay mired in the kitchen or, like Elaine, slip away into a kind of death (even if, in the contemporary model, they still go on living) wherein the usually absent male takes all the blame. Or, more often than we'd like to believe, some women choose to remain in relationships that include physical violence that may lead to their death.

Current statistics indicate that domestic violence is the number one killer of women and that this deadly form of relationship addiction affects women (and batterers) from all walks of life. Cutting to the quick of all the psychological jargon one might heap upon this negative pattern of interaction, the main reasons women stay with potentially murderous partners are low self-esteem, fear, and love.

When a women has low or no self-esteem (for whatever reason—financial, educational, medical, physical, etc.) she is most likely depressed and therefore believes that she is unable to help herself. If she is deathly afraid for her safety and/or that of her children, or if she protects her abusive partner because she loves him, it is also unlikely that she will attempt to change her situation. In all three instances, the intent of the abusive partner is to seek to reinforce insecurity, doubt, and shame in the victim. And so the vicious cycle continues.

The prevaling psychological doctrine is that batterers and the recipients of their tender mercies establish their patterns as a result of learned behavior, meaning that incidents of violence were witnessed and/or experienced during the early years of those involved. This theory holds true in many instances; people can be trained to perform bad deeds as well as good ones. However, there is also reason to believe that a man who beats his girlfriend or wife to the extent of putting her in the hospital or the morgue is just plain crazy.

Although it is of primary importance that women gather the strength and courage to believe in themselves and thus attain freedom from all personal, social, and cultural hindrances, it is also good to be able to recognize the exaggerated behaviors seen in men who are most likely to abuse you. Thererfore, be concerned if the men you choose display the following signs:

Jealousy	Controlling behavior
Quick involvement	Unrealistic expectations
Isolating you from your previous friends	Blaming others for his problems and feelings
Hypersensitivity	Cruelty to animals and/or children
"Playful" force during sex	A history of battering
Verbal abuse	Breaking or striking objects
A "Jekyll and Hyde" personality	Threats of violence
Rigid sex roles	Use of force during an argument

Note that the last four signs are typically present only if the person is a batterer. Three or more of the other behaviors listed above show a strong potential for violence. Should you find yourself trapped in a situation with a Mr. Right who you know in your heart of hearts is Mr. Wrong, please run, don't walk, to the nearest safe place such as a shelter provided for just such a purpose (not to your parents' or a friend's house, where he will be sure to find you). From there, keep right on running—run away from the danger, but do not run from being a woman and do not run from being yourself.

"Femininity" (an ambiguous term at best) is associated in the collective mind with passivity, peace, love, and affection. When women see themselves through the mirror of a man's eyes, they are under pressure to play the role of the love goddess and respond in a way that is sensual, devoted, and appreciative of beauty. But the love goddess is often an indolent and capricious creature, as well as being excessively dependent on relationships. A woman who experiences difficulties in this area is usually so intent upon the "other" that she has trouble developing the self. A woman who has lost her real self may tend to exaggerate the "feminine" aspects of her personality, coming on like Florence Nightingale and then some. Thus men and women alike are compelled to respond to her sympathetic excesses with equal fervor, performing acts of conciliation and caretaking against their better judgment.

When involved in a relationship based on exaggerated passivity, some women just won't say no. They manipulate themselves by being needy, childish, and submissive, while at the same time manipulating others to be competent, supportive, and strong, like good brother Bran. "Pleasers" believe they need continuous help, support, and encouragement. Therefore they seek out "all-powerful" partners or place their misguided trust in anyone who represents authority.

Sometimes such a woman may use theatrics and drama to get her way. The actress makes herself the focal point of attention and uses glamor, charm, emotional outbursts, tears, and seduction as her controlling strategies. In the end, her self-manipulative actions are unrestrained, tempestuous, and undependable.

Exploitation is another tool the "overly feminine" woman or Lover may use to mislead others to be trusting, vulnerable, and open to her own belief system that people are easy prey to a big bad world. Thus her exploitation takes the form of mesmerizing and defrauding her partner/victim.

This, of course, is characteristic of women who are timid in nature—who have little self-esteem and who anticipate rejection. Believing so deeply in a threatening world, they weave for themselves a spell of self-fulfilling prophecy—in the form of big bad men who abuse them with derogatory and fault-finding behavior. These fearful women truly believe that they are unworthy of love and may end up shying away from relationships altogether.

One way or another, the Lover loses her identity, living a sad and sometimes angry half-life in the shadow of a man. The aspect of her individuality—her love goddess soul—that suffers most deeply is that of her sexuality, her erotic nature.

It is not often that a girl or woman will openly express her erotic needs and feelings, her desire for pleasure, or the joy she takes in her own sexuality, from her point of view. A man so dazzled by a woman's beauty that she becomes the object of his passion is compelled to describe the maiden's sensuality. Thus our very image of a girl's adolescent blossoming is itself shaped by the perspective of male longing. This is considered normal in our society.[2]

It may well have been just as normal in medieval Ireland and Wales, for nowhere in the Arthurian legends do we find a purely sexual woman—with the somewhat ambivalent and stormy exception of Queen Morgause. Morgause, though wedded to King Lot of Orkney and mother of many sons (including the famous Sir Gawain), just couldn't say no. She had an affair with her own nephew, King Arthur, and consequently gave birth to the evil Mordred. Later, one of her own sons decapitated her in a fit of rage when he found her in bed with a much younger man. Morgause seems to have been the kind of Lover who simply couldn't lay down the sensual mask of the love goddess to live a real life—at least as she is depicted in Marion Zimmer Bradley's famous novel, *The Mists of Avalon*,[3] wherein she appears as an aging tramp who just can't seem to grow up and find a life that isn't based on her sexual desirability.

So the story of Morgause simply cannot be held up for our admiration as the tale of a wonderfully vigorous, sensual woman. Such tales once existed, however, though the Christian monks who reworked and rewrote the myths into the shape they now bear typically expunged (or, in Morgause's case, darkened) any ribald reference to women who didn't suit their own preconceptions. (They didn't care much for naked women, their long hair shining in the moonlight, dancing around bonfires, hence they simply altered or omitted any such material.)

However, certain aspects of female sensuality remain in the old stories. Maeve, the fierce warrior queen who dominates the Irish epic called

"The Cattle Raid of Cooley," brags to her husband that she has always had "one man waiting in the shadow of another." She praises him for his own lack of jealousy, and shows us what she means by offering her "friendly thighs" to any and every warrior who will take a chance at fighting the invincible Cuchulain. Earlier in the same epic, the princess Nes asks the druid Cathbach what the present day is most auspicious for. When the druid answers "Conceiving a great king," Nes grabs him and and immediately gets to work, inasmuch as he is (as she herself puts it) "the only man in sight." Thus she becomes the mother of the great Connor mac Nessa.

Another darker and more profound vision of sex survives in the tale of Blodeuwedd.[4] She was a "Maid of Flowers," a soft and gentle creature whose sensuality was entirely at the service of men and who had no life of her own.

Or did she? Simulated perfection has its price.

The sorceress Arianrhod, Lady of the Silver Wheel, declared that her son, Llew Llaw Gyffes, would "never have a wife of the race that is now on this earth." So Llew's magician uncle, Gwydion of the Magic Harp, paid a visit to old Math, son of Mathonwy, an even greater magician. The two of them contrived, through magic and enchantment, to conjure up a wife for Llew out of flowers. Robert Graves purports to find the tale of Blodeuwedd's birth embedded in an old Welsh poem called "The Battle of the Trees":

> *Neither of mother or father,*
> *When I was made,*
> *Was my blood or body;*
> *...When I was made*
> *Of the blossoms of the nettle,*
> *Of the waters of the ninth wave,*
> *I was spell-bound by Math*
> *Before I became immortal.*
> *I was spell-bound by Gwydion,*
> *Great enchanter of the Britons...*[5]

She was without any visible flaw, the perfect Donna Reed prototype—beautiful, smiling, supportive, contented, giving, and feminine. She was Good with a capital "G."

There was only one problem. She wasn't human. How could she be? She had been created by powerful men who formulated her in the image of their own desires, feelings, and ideas about what the Lover should be.

Llew was smitten. In the beginning, Blodeuwedd followed the ritual of courtship mindlessly and slept with Llew after the feast. They went to a place called Mur Castell and set up court.

One day, while Llew was "away on business" (a term that is still both familiar and suspicious), Blodeuwedd was stirring about outside and heard the blast of a horn. She saw a tired, bloodied stag go by. The unfortunate beast was pursued by dogs, huntsmen, and a troop of men on foot. Blodeuwedd sent a boy to inquire as to whose company it was. "This is Goronwy Pebyr, lord of Penllyn," was the answer.

When Goronwy finished his business with the stag, Blodeuwedd invited him in. They sat down to meat, and the moment Blodeuwedd looked at him she was filled with desire. Something deep inside her—the raw, elemental lustiness that ensouled and empowered her, and of which she had until now been totally unaware—suddenly woke up. Was this not a portion of her birthright as a Lover? Had she not received certain "gifts" from her creators, Math and Gwydion? Surely this ecstasy signified that she too was at home in the ecstatic starlight of the Milky Way, called Gwydion's Castle for the great magician who had made her.

> In myriads of secrets,
> I am as learned as Math...
> I know the star-knowledge
> Of stars before the earth [was made],
> Whence I was born,
> How many worlds there are.[6]

When she blossomed into the fullness of her innermost self, Blodeuwedd came upon her own inner muse. Like contemporary women who awaken at last from the dream of a perfect marriage, perfect devotion, perfect wife, perfect life, she was able to hear the eternal music playing in her soul, to sing and dance to its harmony and rhythm.

Yet this blossoming of self arose because of another individual—the violent, lusty Goronwy Pebyr. Like all good Lovers, she was still seeking positive reinforcement in the magic mirror of relationships. She had found the muse, but did not yet recognize that she was the muse. She was writing the poetry of her life from a man's point of view—the man with whom she had most suddenly "fallen in love." She wasn't really being true to the vital essence of herself. Wise, loving, forbidding, changeable—Blodeuwedd was the moon, but the moon only half-full and hidden behind a cloud.

Let us remember that Blodeuwedd was created and awakened by men. Her undeveloped personality could respond only to the primal instincts and emotions that ruled her being. She had acted upon the muse within herself, and soon she would dance over the flames of a sacrificial fire, her soul crying out for death and blood, without knowing why. The sensual power that lies at the core of the Lover's myth is a wild and elemental force indeed.

Her heart was filled with great joy, affection, and love. Blodeuwedd did not delay in sharing her feelings with Goronwy; they slept together that night. Two days later, as Goronwy prepared to take his leave, Blodeuwedd vowed to extract from Llew (under the pretense of genuine concern and loving care) the secret of the magic that could work his death.

Blodeuwedd celebrated Llew's return with talk, song, feasting, and lovemaking. When he was properly vulnerable, she got the information she was after. Llew could only be killed by magical means, for he would never be slain while "indoors or out of doors, on horse or on foot." Blodeuwedd persuaded him to demonstrate, and Llew took up his position under a well-thatched roof without any walls, one foot on a cauldron by a river and the other resting on the back of a goat. Goronwy Pebyr was there, and thrust a spear into Llew's back.

When Gwydion discovered Blodeuwedd's treachery, he hunted her down just as Goronwy had hunted the stag. He pursued her up a mountain and over the Cynfael River. When Blodeuwedd and her maidens reached the lake, all were drowned save she. Then Gwydion overtook her. He did not kill her, but instead bade her go in the form of a bird that would never show its face by the light of day. The name of that bird was *tylluan*, the owl, and since one of Llew's other names was Huan, Blodeuwedd was sometimes called Twyll Huan, which means "the deceiving of Huan."[7]

The owl is a bird of prey, easily distinguished by its large head, eyes surrounded by stiff-feathered disks, a short, hooked beak, feathered legs with sharp talons, and soft plumage which permits noiseless flight. Its habits are nocturnal, its appearance solemn. When Blodeuwedd, once a love goddess, was transformed, she became the owl of wisdom.

However, owls have another aspect. They are most active on moon-lit nights in November and then remain quiet through February. Their nests bear the feral scent of carrion; they have a taste for mice and their yellow eyes have a fiery glow in the dark. In many cultures, the owl symbolizes death, night, cold, and passivity. It is often associated with sorcery of a dark and shadowy nature. The owl may serve as a classic witches' familiar, a creature with which the very life and soul of the witch are united. In fact, such an intimate union is established between the two that the death of one may entail the death of the other. This alliance brings great power, which may then be turned to the witch's advantage, especially in revenge or counter-magic.

In northern India, it is believed that eating the eyeballs of the owl will enable you to see in the dark. Some Native Americans refer to the owl as "night eagle," for the night, the dark, and all things unseen are the owl's friends. Despite the owl's reputation for wisdom, some Native Americans fear those who possess owl medicine, because even as the owl can prevent you from being deceived, it can also serve those who use deception and sorcery against you. The Maya, as well as some Plains Indian tribes, believe that to hear an owl hooting in the night is a warning of death, which reminds one of the Celtic belief that the rasping cry of the scritch-owl is prophetic of a king's death.[8]

Owls are messengers of the death goddesses: Hecate, Athene (in her original Underworld aspect), Persephone, Arianrhod, Cerridwen. Blodeuwedd may have been created as a love goddess, but she bears the imprint of a darker goddess within.

Let us remember that Blodeuwedd was not actually destroyed for her evil deed, but transformed into the diametrical opposite of her previous self. From a meek, gentle, smiling, benign, beautiful, and perfect mate, she became a solitary night predator, maw gaping in silent flight, screech cutting through the forest. In a positive sense, we may say that she became assertive, independent, self-realized—and wise.

Nor was Llew really dead. The moment the spear pierced him, he was transformed into an eagle (bird of shamans) and flew away, later to be healed of his wound and restored to human shape by Gwydion.[9] So by bringing about Llew's apparent death, Blodeuwedd actually brought both Llew and herself back to life! They were grown by the experience to bring to consciousness the full extent of their individuality and adulthood. A woman's path often leads her through death then back into life. This is something we must remember when we come, at last, to dwell for a while in Caer Arianrhod, at the center of the Silver Wheel.

Blodeuwedd is sometimes called the May Bride, because she, like Freya and Holda of Norse myth, or Rhea and Artemis in the Mediterranean, brought about the sacrifice of the sacred king (Llew) through the medium of a sacred marriage. Such goddesses are often depicted as dark enchantresses of frightening countenance—black-faced and long-haired, with a raven flying above them, a hare running ahead, a hound at their side, a veil over their faces, and a goat, perhaps, as a mount.[10] Blodeuwedd's connection with goats is apparent in the story itself, for a goat figures in the murder scene.

Thus Blodeuwedd is also an aspect of yet another goddess, perhaps the oldest of all. Poet and scholar Robert Graves calls her the White Goddess because, for him, she is primarily the goddess of the moon. However, archaeologist Marija Gimbutas regards the White Goddess primarily as a goddess of death and rebirth. Gimbutas discovered her "lady in white" while excavating the oldest settled villages of Europe—those of the Balkans and the Ukraine that date back to about 5000 B.C. She believes our archetypal image of death as a spectral woman in white (like the Irish banshee) goes all the way back to the Neolithic.[11] This goddess appears again and again throughout ancient Europe as the Queen of the Dead, though the White Lady may occasionally be seen in black when she comes forth (usually as a raven) to gather the souls of the dead. One of her birds, of course, is the owl. Another is the raven, associated with Badbh and the Morrigan, the Celtic goddesses who retrieved the bodies of slain warriors from the battlefield. Branwen's name means "White Raven," and this was presumably the title by which the love goddess was known in Wales and Cornwall. Behind every love goddess lies the goddess of death.

Blodeuwedd is like many women today, for what is common, but wholly unnatural, to them is the silence that surrounds them—a silence of noiseless flight—and the shroud which covers them like the dark face of the Death Goddess or the deep forest wherein she dwells. In Saudi Arabia, the shroud that covers women is quite literal, for a woman may not be seen in public without a black, full-length outer garment to cover her clothes and a veil made of black fabric to cover her face. Often the Saudi woman is confined to her home and may travel only when accompanied by a man who is her father, husband, brother, or uncle. Female circumcision is still practiced in extremely traditional Muslim families throughout the Middle East. This barbaric custom, occurring when a girl has reached the age of puberty, includes removal (via scissors and a razor wielded by the local barber) of some or all of the external female genitalia, including the clitoris, the labia minora, and the labia majora! If these practices are not enough to ensure that women remain silent and in the dark, there is always the woman's room, a tiny, dark, padded cell inside the home wherein a "disobedient" woman may be confined and isolated from all human contact for a part or all of her life, should her closest male relative see fit.[12]

So, like those of the owl, the movements of women are quiet. Like Flower Maidens, they can go for a long time without expressing themselves. Are we silent because we fear punishment and rejection for expressing our feelings and desires in words? How many times have we attempted to tell our lovers what pleases us in bed, only to be shunned, ignored, or outright abused for our efforts? When we attempt to verbally define the erotic, passionate beings we really are, we are often condemned as obscene, vulgar, cold, threatening, predatory, unfeminine, and unreal. Our silence substantiates us, makes us real and viable within the context of society—though not within the context of our souls. It proves to one and all that a woman is "tame"—our collective notion of the perfect love goddess. But women are not what they seem, for the Queen of the Dead, the oldest goddess of all, lies deep within all women.

A woman may have emerged from the great barrow mound of the collective mind, and she may be enjoying some success at walking the Silver Wheel of life. After all, Rhiannon emerged from the mound of the Gorsedd Arberth wearing a veil like the women of Saudi Arabia. Unlike those women, however, she raised her veil, revealing her full empowerment to all who would see her. Perhaps in this way she declared to Pwyll that although she wanted to be his wife, she would not be subjugated. Sooner or later a woman must return from where she came, deep into the heart of all things, and face the old white crone of death and rebirth. It does her no good to try and avoid the old one. It is better to embrace her, for only by so doing may a woman learn her wisdom. Only by so doing may she avoid being seized by the death crone—who becomes very angry when she is ignored or not honored properly. How, then, does one make friends with the White Lady? We shall learn the answer to that question when at last we enter the labyrinth of the Underworld.

A Lover, being, as she is, a woman of flowers, has trouble facing the Death Goddess. She lives in an artificial world of sweetness and light. This makes the old one angry, for her own special brand of wisdom—the deep knowledge of the dark places—has been ignored. Because the woman of flowers lacks a strong sense of individuality, she may find herself possessed by a force greater than any individuality—the archetypal power of the death crone.

This, then, is the darkness that lies at the heart of the Flower Maiden, and why it is unhealthy for her to allow men or society to fashion for her a personality made out of sweetness and roses. The longer her rage fails to find its proper expression, the angrier the Death Goddess becomes. And then she takes over.

The archetype of the Flower Maiden gone mad is one which has begun to surface with disturbing force in our own society. Take, for example, the case of Tracy Lippard—who, as a beauty queen, might almost be defined as a "professional Flower Maiden." Tracy briefly dated a certain Todd Scott, who later became involved with a girl named Melissa Weikle. When Melissa became pregnant, Todd decided to devote his energies to his relationship with her.

Tracy was annoyed. After crowning her successor to the title of Miss Williamsburg, Virginia, and singing Whitney Houston's "I'm Every Woman" and Celine Dion's "The Power of Love," she armed herself with a gun, a hammer, a butcher knife, and some lighter fluid. She drove her red Toyota toward West Virginia, home of Melissa Weikle, and—after receiving a ticket for going 80 in a 65 MPH zone—replaced her Virginia license plates with stolen New York tags. She knocked on the door of the Weikle home in Lewisburg, and told Rodney Weikle, Melissa's father, that she needed to use the phone. Weikle led Tracy into the kitchen, where she pulled out a hammer and hit him in the head.

Unfortunately for Tracy, Weikle was a former Secret Service agent. Instead of collapsing, he twirled her around and put her in a headlock. Tracy then attempted to pull her gun, but Weikle's wife Carlynn arrived to help her husband wrestle Tracy to the ground.

As of this writing, Tracy Lippard is appealing her conviction on charges of attempted murder.

Another, more celebrated, contemporary case is that of Lorena Bobbit, a pretty, dark-haired manicurist from South America who claimed that she was physically, emotionally, and verbally abused for many years by her ex-Marine husband, John Wayne Bobbit. She claimed that one night, during one of his bouts of insobriety, he forced Lorena to have sex and then fell asleep. According to Lorena, all of this was nothing new; but this time something in her snapped. When she went to the kitchen to get a drink of water, she spied a paring knife. Picking it up, she walked into the bedroom, lifted the blanket, and cut off John Wayne's penis. She then proceeded to get into her car, penis in hand, and drive down the parkway for a while until, realizing that she still clutched the severed member, she threw it out the window where it landed on the shoulder of the road, to be surgically re-attached later on. Both parties were acquitted of all charges lodged against them, though Lorena was required to undergo psychiatric examination before she was free to establish a psychic phone line out of Florida. Meanwhile, John Wayne played out his cowboy fantasy, hooked up with a Las Vegas showgirl, and has made millions of dollars lecturing about the fate of his penis.

Because she was from a country that values passivity in women, putting her at a cultural disadvantage, Lorena was another fair example of a Flower Maiden. John Wayne was able to play Pygmalion to her Galatea, initiating her into American life as the ideal (or his ideal) American wife. Though there was no Goronwy Pebyr to spur her on, Lorena, deprived of individuality, found her own way to the vengeful Death Goddess and was compelled to (dare we say?) alter the course of both their lives. The sacred king in the sacred marriage was sacrificed by the May Bride.

Thus complete absorption in a relationship, giving rise to a loss of individuality, can lead women to truly archetypal depths of rage. A sense of self is the only solution. In order to function in any spiritual sense, they must cultivate self-esteem so that they experience genuine pleasure in the company of others—without feeling the need to pattern their actions or responses through immature behavior in order to feel worthy of love. They need to question their relationships and the ability to grow within the confines of intimate partnerships. Most women are sufficiently aware to know when a relationship is destructive and are able to let go without falling to pieces, because they have taken the time to develop their own friends and interests. They must learn to place value on inner peace in order to be capable of living in true harmony, balance, and intimacy with others. Self-exploration, self-discovery, and self-protection are keynotes to spiritual growth and well-being. If women are to act as channels of heartfelt energy, they must accept themselves totally by choosing to look within for validation, rather than to another for a sense of self-worth.

According to an old story, King Arthur became lost in the forest one day. While trying to decide which path would take him home, he came upon a hideously ugly woman. Her skin was wrinkled and pockmarked, her nose twisted and long, and her teeth a nice mossy green.

Although she was so very ugly, she seemed harmless enough, so King Arthur approached her to ask for directions (a tremendously humble act for a man, who usually reveals his geographic confusion only to male gas station attendants).

"I will tell you how to get home," said the Loathly Lady, "but in turn you must grant me a favor."

"Anything," replied the king, perhaps a little too quickly, so anxious was he to be on his way and far from her unseemly presence.

After giving him directions, the Loathly Lady proceeded to ask her favor: that one of the king's knights should marry her and become her husband.

Damn, thought the king as he hurried back to his castle. *What have I done? None of my men deserve this....*

But upon his return home, his knights were so grateful to have him back that one of them, Sir Gawain—at that time the youngest and most handsome—volunteered to marry the woman, sight unseen. *How bad could she be?* he thought.

So Sir Gawain and the Loathly Lady were married. All the king's court, including Gawain, were indeed appalled by her frightful appearance. However, Sir Gawain was too much the courteous knight to show the fear, depression, and downright disgust he felt in the presence of his loathesome bride.

But she knew how he felt, all the same. That night, when they were finally ensconced in the wedding chamber, Sir Gawain stood looking sadly at the huge marriage bed looming before him. *I have fought many battles,* he thought, *but none so great as this.* The Loathly Lady was sitting at the dressing table, combing out the drab gray nest of her hair. Seeing his crestfallen reflection in the mirror, she called him to her side.

"My husband," said she, trying not to notice as Sir Gawain winced at the possessive pronoun. He turned around and, lo and behold, the bald spots, nose warts, drooping eyelids and hunchback were gone. The most drop-dead gorgeous maiden he had ever set eyes on now stood before him with a youthful, lithe, and comely form, long wavy hair the color of golden wheat, a peaches-and-cream complexion, and long-lashed azure blue eyes that mirrored the sky in autumn. Sir Gawain stood with his mouth open as the No-Longer-Loathly Lady explained to him that she had been put under a spell, and only his correct response to the question she would now pose could free her—and thus render her beautiful forever.

She asked him, "Would it be better if I were beautiful by night and ugly by day, or beautiful by day and ugly by night?"

"Well," he replied, "perhaps you should be beautiful by night."

"Ah," said she. "That would benefit you when we are together in our bedchamber, but by day all would see my loathesomeness and I would still suffer from ridicule, abhorrence, and jests."

"Mmmm, I see your point," said Sir Gawain. "In that case I think it would be better if you were beautiful by day and ugly by night."

The lady gave this response very little thought before she replied, "This would serve you well insofar as I would then be a credit to your reputation, but the evenings would be a gloomy affair, for you would still find me hideous and reject me."

Having failed to hit upon the correct answer, Sir Gawain was by this time becoming exasperated. In frustration, he blurted out, "Well then, do as you please!"

The lady beamed at Sir Gawain with the most radiant of smiles, threw her arms around him and cried, "Oh thank you, my husband! Because you have given me my own way, the spell is now broken and I will remain beautiful both by day and by night forevermore."

What does every woman want? To have her own way.

She feels ugly when her desires are not expressed and fulfilled, beautiful when she is free to do and be who she is and have what she needs and wants. Her problems arise when she depends on others to give her her way via their approval of her actions. For this reason, women may strive to be perfect, to be nice, to be "good." However, their concept of "good" can modify and diminish the self, which they sacrifice, abnegate, restrain, contain, or deny in an effort to hold themselves down, back, or in abeyance. When they have succeeded in being selfless, they have perhaps attained the highest possible goal in fulfilling the expectations and needs of others.[13] How can they be content when there is nothing but a hollow void where the soul should be? They are sucked inside themselves, as if through a black hole in space, losing their femininity in the process. Some wear more makeup and lower-cut, tighter clothing in an attempt to effect a balance. Others crop their hair, don combat boots, and smoke cigars in an effort to assert the self they have lost. Sexual preferences are not at issue here. What is at issue is that many women are hurt and angry. They aren't getting what they want from others, and worse, they aren't giving themselves what they want, either. Like the Loathly Lady, they feel physically, emotionally, intellectually, or spiritually deformed, bewitched by a malevolent power that holds them spellbound against their will. Unlike the Loathly Lady, however, they cannot afford to wait around for a handsome knight to come along, marry them (warts and all), and break the spell. In the modern world, a woman must do this for herself.

So how do they go about getting what they want (short of undergoing plastic surgery or inviting a spirit "walk-in" to take over)? They need to end the tug-of-war between personal contentment and compromise in their relationships. To do this, they must decide whether they want to continue being "good" (i.e. chaste, pure, silent, and pleasing) or begin being "bad"— looking, dressing, speaking, and doing precisely as they wish, for themselves and no one else. Does this include their sexuality, their ability to express themselves as sexy, erotic beings? You bet it does. How can a woman be primal, pagan, and wild if she buries her passions, desires, and feelings? Do you know any wolves who do that? Nope. While functioning in a relatively structured, civilized wolf society, they eat when they're hungry, bite when they're mad, rut when they're aroused, and sleep when they're tired. Granted, they don't have to work a nine-to-five job, but the idea of "Do what thou wilt an it harm none" is implicit in their lifestyle. The rules are created for women who want approval, not for women who want things for themselves. "Good" means "good for everybody else." "Bad" means "getting what you want."

In order to bring about this dramatic change in consciousness, to move from ugly to beautiful or "good" to "bad," it's necessary that women give up the following self-destructive ideas:

> The idea that entering into a relationship with a man or any other individual requires a drastic personal transformation because a woman cannot be herself and be loved at the same time.

> The idea that, following the change which will render her "loathly," the person for whom a woman went through so much trouble will still be able to see the real her.

> The idea that if a man fails to recognize who she is, or if he doesn't like what he sees, she's about to become an endangered species.

The idea that a woman should be without malice, no matter what happens; that she should be grateful, selfless, yielding, forgiving and, above all, silent—that she will be "good."

The idea that a woman's willingness to be silent and loathly will qualify her for the role of paragon of perfection.

Changing old systems of belief and patterns of behavior takes time. One phase of the process of awakening, of entering into womanhood, is recognizing those moments when the wind of a higher power—the wind of the Otherworld—is blowing through our lives, seeking to move us to a new place, a new level of awareness. How many women are still stuck in childhood fantasy and trauma? How many women still carry the pain of the verbal, physical, or mental abuse they may have suffered on into adulthood? Why can't they let go?

Most of us associate love either with idyllic romance or with mundane security. Either way, we somehow believe—despite our past failures—that love will bring a sense of wholeness, fulfillment, and inspired creativity. This is love in an elevated, perfect state. For the masses, love is still about sex, pure and simple. Without love there would be no procreation, and therefore no birth, no life.

And therefore no death, either.

Fear of death—any kind of death—lies at the root of all material, emotional, mental, and spiritual attachment. When we try to die a little and release old patterns, our whole way of being is disrupted. Our security and comfort are threatened; it's easier to hang on to an old, outmoded form, even if that form is painful. The French call orgasm "the little death," and we realize death every time we make love, its dark approach shrouded in orgasmic pleasure. When it arrives in this form, death leads us to birth and thus back to life again. Death cannot exist without desire, without relationship, without love. Nor can love exist without change and the willingness to let go. The change that comes with love's awakening can come at any time; love and death are intertwined as the ultimate sacrifice, the source of all life on earth. The cup that Branwen the love goddess gave to Tristan and Iseult contained both love and death. During such a time, a woman is tested and tried, incubated, metamorphosed. The new sense of self which emerges with change may bring with it the gift of self-forgiveness, the release of creativity, and the recovery of what was lost.

A woman owes it to herself to have alone time, to ask for what she wants, to request information, to make mistakes and be forgiven when she does less than she is humanly capable of doing. She has the right to say what she means and not feel guilty, to experience and express emotions, to enjoy sex, to eat well, to be successful, to be appreciated. A woman has the right to feel good about herself without recrimination from others, and without compromising herself by acting out negative patterns of manipulation. A woman has the right to be treated with respect and to promote self-respect and self-esteem, provided no one is hurt in the process.

Take the following quiz to determine whether or not you demonstrate the Lover's darker characteristics of feigned femininity.

	YES	NO
1. Are you passive and peace-loving?	_____	_____
2. Are you demonstrative in your affections toward others?	_____	_____
3. Are you devoted and loyal in your relationships?	_____	_____
4. Are you artistically inclined or appreciative of beauty?	_____	_____
5. Do you consider yourself a sensualist?	_____	_____
6. Are you sometimes indolent or lazy?	_____	_____
7. Is making a decision difficult for you?	_____	_____
8. Are you fickle and/or capricious in your emotional commitments to others?	_____	_____
9. Do you need to be "in relationship" in order to maintain your sense of emotional equilibrium?	_____	_____
10. Do you prefer to have others take responsibility for your needs, wants, and desires?	_____	_____
11. When left to your own devices, do you feel that you are somehow separated from reality?	_____	_____
12. Do you often attempt to please others in an effort to act submissive and/or conciliatory?	_____	_____
13. Do you allow others to use you in ways that are hurtful to you?	_____	_____

	YES	NO
14. Have you ever allowed another to verbally or physically abuse you?	_____	_____
15. Do you take secret pleasure in feeling hurt or rejected?	_____	_____
16. Do you think you are "perfect" and therefore unattainable?	_____	_____
17. Do you feel that you lack spiritual, mental, emotional, or physical boundaries?	_____	_____
18. Are you totally consumed or preoccupied by your intimate relationships?	_____	_____
19. Are you possessive or do you desire to be possessed by your significant other?	_____	_____
20. Is your need to be "in relationship" compulsive in nature?	_____	_____

Scoring

Questions 1 through 5 represent positive relationship patterns. A majority of "yes" answers in this area indicates a healthy expression of traditional femininity in relationships. A majority of "no" answers in this section suggests imbalance surrounding how you perceive yourself in relationship issues.

Questions 6 through 15 spotlight the afflicted feminine nature. A majority of "yes" answers here means that you have work to do in the area of self and other. A majority of "no" answers signifies a strong individuality with a wholesome view of self and relationships.

Questions 16 through 20 indicate challenging relationship patterns. A majority of "yes" answers in this section indicates the need for heightened self-esteem and self-protection, while a majority of "no" answers suggests a secure and balanced response to the needs of others.

Endnotes

1. Gantz, *Mabinogion*, 67-82.

2. Dalma Heyn, *The Erotic Silence of the American Wife* (New York: Turtle Bay Books, 1992).

3. New York: Alfred A. Knopf, 1983.

4. Gantz, *Mabinogion,* 111-17.

5. Quoted in Graves, *The White Goddess,* 33-34.

6. Ibid.

7. Ibid., 85.

8. Frazier, *The Golden Bough,* 496, 684; and Graves, *The White Goddess,* 211.

9. Llew's story is one of death, rebirth, and initiation. For the male point of view, see Johnson and Elsbeth, *The Grail Castle,* Chapters 3 and 4.

10. Graves, *The White Goddess,* 303-304.

11. Marija Gimbutas, *The Language of the Goddess* (San Francisco: Harper and Row, 1989), 209ff.

12. Jean Sasson, *Princess Sultana's Daughters* (New York: Doubleday, 1994).

13. Heyn, *Erotic Silence of the American Wife.*

CHAPTER FOUR

The Goddess of the Land

When a woman, as mother, has faced the Old Death Goddess, she is transformed into a Goddess of Sovereignty who knows how to command, how to fight, how to exult in the wild joy of Nature and love.

THREE YEARS PASSED, and Rhiannon had yet to provide Pwyll with offspring—this, at least, was how the men of Dyved felt about Pwyll's lack of an heir. They suggested that, should the situation remain thus, it might behoove Pwyll to take a second wife. They agreed to talk about it again in council come the end of the year.

But before year's end, Rhiannon gave birth to a beautiful baby boy in the place called Arberth. Six women were brought in to attend her and her newborn son. They watched for part of the evening, but soon all fell asleep, including Rhiannon, who was exhausted from her labor.

Upon cock-crow the next morning, the women awoke to find Rhiannon still fast asleep—and the baby missing from her side.

"Alas," said one of the women, "the child is lost!"

"Aye," said another, "and they will put us to death because of it!"

"What shall we do?" wondered yet another, her fear rising at the prospect of an untimely end.

The cleverest among them replied, "I know of a stag hound bitch with pups. Let us take some of the pups and kill them, and smear blood on Rhiannon's face and hands. And let us throw the bones of the pups before her, and we will swear that she killed her own son in a maddened frenzy. If the six of us all insist that this is true, no one will believe her, for she will stand all alone."

The women agreed that this was sound counsel, and acted on the plan to save their lives.

When Rhiannon awoke, she asked for her child. And the women told her that her child was dead and that she herself had killed him, and, pity them, they were covered with blows and bruises from their struggle to save him from her vicious onslaught.

Rhiannon knew the women were lying. "Poor creatures," she said, "the gods know the truth, and that you accuse me falsely out of fear. Don't worry, I will protect you from harm."

But the women refused to change their story, despite all Rhiannon's sympathy, bargaining, pleading, and cajoling.

The tale of the six women spread through the land like wildfire. All the chief men heard it and requested that Pwyll put his wife away for committing such an outrageous crime. Much to his credit, however, Pwyll stood by his woman. He insisted that because Rhiannon had indeed given him offspring, he would not put her away; instead, he would have her serve penance, on the off-chance that she had done wrong.

Upon cock-crow the next morning, the women awoke to find Rhiannon still fast asleep—and the baby missing ....

With her teachers and Druids all around her, Rhiannon decided to serve out the penance rather than dispute with the women who had lied against her. As her punishment, she was to remain in the court at Arberth until the end of seven years, and to sit every day near a horse block outside the palace gate. From this place she was to tell the story of her evil deed to all who should come there and who did not yet know of it—and, to every guest or stranger who would allow it, she would offer a ride to court upon her back.

And thus a part of the year went past....

Motherhood is a serious business, though Rhiannon's story[1] is a great deal more intense than most. Then again, she is a woman of faery, and though the earth-plane process of childbirth seemed to come easily enough, the aftermath proved difficult. In modern terms, we might suspect that Rhiannon suffered one hell of a postpartum depression.

If a few psychologists had been present during this incident in pre-Christian Wales (which, thank the gods, they were not), they would probably have questioned whether or not Rhiannon had a good relationship with her own mother. We may safely assume that she did, for Rhiannon, as part of the Triple Goddess, is her own mother! So perhaps the question should be: Did Rhiannon have a good relationship with herself?

For Rhiannon, as for many women, a fine line existed between fact and fancy regarding the circumstances surrounding the birthing process. The birth of a child will trigger vast worldly concerns in a woman's mind as well as sweeping hormonal changes that affect both her emotions and her body. On spiritual levels, there exists a deep connectedness with all of life, as a woman giving birth is wholly immersed in the miracle of procreation. When that momentary glimpse of the Otherworld occurs, then who among us can say what reality is? Does it wreak havoc in our lives, or, because we have seen a wonder, lighten the burden of the future?

Let us examine this powerful, universal concept called "mother." Maternal consciousness is primarily concerned with relations and the earth, as women share an observant sensitivity to and acceptance of natural phenomena. Therefore, symbols we associate with the Earth Mother may include water, stone, caves, the home, night, depth, strength, and wisdom.[2] She may also embody ideas associated with fecundity, abundance, beauty, love, affection, harmony, and peace.

And yet no two mothers are alike. Mothers come in various shapes and sizes, some with ambivalent temperaments. We have all heard about Mother Nature, a name that conjures up the image of a universal, life-giving, all-embracing goddess. But Nature can be terrible as well, and the Terrible Mother is another image we must reckon with—most especially in our present tale, for Rhiannon has been accused of devouring her child.

The Terrible or Devouring Mother is perhaps best known in her Hindu incarnation as Kali the Destroyer. Furnished with a pair of fangs, wearing a necklace of skulls and a belt made of severed human arms, she dances out of the fire with her scythe upraised, ready to seek and destroy. Utterly impervious to all our hopes and pleas, she wreaks her vengeance on one and all.

But we have met this goddess before, have we not?

She is, of course, the White Lady or Old European Death Goddess. Blodeuwedd, the May Bride and charming flower girl we met in the previous chapter, bore the inner imprint of the Dark Mother. Living on the surface of reality, Blodeuwedd failed to plumb her own inner depths, and paid the penalty, for the Ancient One came storming out of the depths to meet her, calling for murder and mayhem.

Now here she comes again, to bring a similar quantity of murder and mayhem into Rhiannon's life. If the Death Goddess lies beneath the smiling facade of every love goddess, she lurks beneath the nurturing breasts of every mother as well. And indeed, in the Hellenistic mystery schools, returning to the Mother was equivalent to spiritual death.

In Celtic myth, the raven was one of the most important symbols of the Terrible Mother, for the raven is a scavenger who devours corpses on the battlefield. The Irish goddess called the Morrigan, who often appears in the form of a raven, constitutes one such example of this dark side of the maternal nature.

But what about the Death Goddess as a mother?

Throughout Britain and Ireland, one occasionally finds carvings of female figures whose mouths are twisted with anger or pain and who squat upon the ground, displaying their genitalia. These carvings are most commonly found upon the walls of (can you believe it?) medieval churches. No one really knows what these female figures are supposed to represent. An Irish peasant, queried by folklorists, said they were called "sheela-na-gigs"—unfortunately, no one quite agrees on the meaning of that term. Celtic scholar Anne Ross believes the sheela-na-gigs are related to the old Celtic battle goddess in her crone or hag aspect.[3] This, then, is the Old Death Goddess once again.

But what about her unusual posture? Is she, in fact, merely indulging in an exhibitionistic romp?

The squatting pose characteristic of the sheela-na-gig is found in other, more ancient contexts—notably in the early farming villages of the Balkans which date back to the so-called Goddess cultures of circa 5000 B.C. and which also provide us with our first images of the "lady in white." In the Balkans, however, a stylized toad is often carved in the squatting position, and the toad was a manifestation of the Goddess in her birth-giving aspect (carved toads still serve as votive offerings in remote European communities, placed in the church to ensure childbirth; eating toad's meat was an old country charm to ease labor pains).[4]

Is the sheela-na-gig giving birth, her mouth twisted in the pain and suffering of labor? And is such an activity appropriate to the battle goddess as hag?

In an earlier chapter, we met King Connor of Ulster, leader of the Red Branch heroes and frustrated suitor of the beautiful Deirdre. During Connor's time, a farmer named Crunniuc, a lonely widower, received a visit from the Otherworld. A beautiful woman by the name of Macha appeared in his home one day and immediately took up residence, cooking and cleaning and behaving like an altogether perfect wife. She told Crunniuc that only one taboo would be laid upon him which, if broken, would result in her departure: he was never to speak of her among other people.

One day, Crunniuc went to attend a festival among the Red Branch champions of Ulster. Macha warned him that he must never boast of her in the presence of those there, and he assured her that there would be no problem. At the fair, horse races were in progress, and King Connor's steeds were on a winning streak. Indulging in a fine boast (a practice which warriors in all the Indo-European mythologies seemed to regard as an art form), Connor affirmed that no creature alive could beat his horses.

Then Crunniuc, who may have been a bit drunk, remembered Macha's Otherworldly powers and shouted out that his wife could run faster than Connor's precious horses. For his moment of indiscretion, Crunniuc was seized and held captive while Macha was sent for. Connor was in a capricious mood—either Macha could race against the king's horses, or Crunniuc could be executed. It was that simple.

Unfortunately, Macha was pregnant at the time. She begged to be allowed to give birth before the race, but Connor was unyielding. And so she began to run.

Macha won the race, but collapsed into the agony of childbirth, delivering twin boys right there on the ground. It killed her, but with her dying curse she decreed that the heroes of the Red Branch, whenever they were in their hour of greatest need, would fall ill with the pangs of childbirth for five whole days! (A fitting curse to place upon a bunch of warlike men, some would say.) The capital of Ulster was ever afterward known as Emain Macha, the "Twins of Macha."[5]

Now, this Macha is an interesting character. The same Professor Ross who asserts that the sheela-na-gig is none other than the old Celtic battle goddess says that the battle goddess is another aspect of the Triple Goddess, for she appears in three different aspects: the Morrigan, Badbh (a name meaning "battle raven"), and Macha.[6]

Both the Morrigan and Badbh took the raven as their totem, but Macha took the horse, as did Rhiannon and Epona. Like Rhiannon, Macha is linked with horses (for that matter, so are her sons, for the Divine Twins tend to be horsemen in most Indo-European mythologies). In pain and suffering she gives birth, twisted with pain and rage like the sheela-na-gig. She delivers a curse. And she is none other than the Celtic battle goddess, who also appears as the death hag.

The Celts, then, like other peoples, knew the Death Goddess as a Terrible Mother. If we look back upon the story of Blodeuwedd—who was the Death Goddess as Terrible Lover—the message becomes a bit more clear: If a woman enters into motherhood without sufficient self-knowledge, she is likely to have an unpleasant encounter with the Old Death Mother. If she doesn't travel back into the great barrow mound of the Otherworld to hone her spirit senses, she's likely to devour her children out of ignorance.

This, in psychological terms, is what happens to Rhiannon.

The Terrible Mother may seem to be indifferent to human suffering, yet she, like all mothers, dwells in the great barrow mound of the collective unconscious, on the night side of our existence, and hence she is the source of all things, the very water of life. During pregnancy the fetus is safely harbored in the amniotic fluid. Suspended in its own "water of life" in the uterine sac, the child-to-be floats in a benign darkness, the womb of the great universal mother. Thus the child who will be born into this world begins its journey in the Otherworld, wherein there is no time, and where space is a warm nurturing vessel set sail upon lifetimes to dream emotions, feelings, and memories. In symbolic language, the fetus is alive within the body of the moon, since the mean duration of pregnancy is nine lunar months, the number of the Triple Goddess tripled.[7] Like the moon reflecting the light of the sun, the pregnant woman reflects her sentiments, sensitivities, intuitions, securities, comforts, and ancestries onto her offspring.

She may also reflect her prejudices, blind spots, morbid imaginings, insecurities, discomforts, and family karma. From just such an imprint on the child's mind, the Terrible Mother is made manifest.

One of the most terrifying (or terrible) mothers in all of Celtic myth is Cerridwen. Feminist scholars have long suspected that Cerridwen was once a more benign goddess, the keeper of the cauldron of death and rebirth. Be that as it may, it is also possible that her more frightening aspects indicate that she is but another incarnation of the Old Death Goddess, the primordial spirit of death and resurrection who appears in ancient shamanic lore and whom, in another work,[8] we have named the Bone Mother.

In any event, there is one surviving story (omitted from most versions of the *Mabinogion* but included in one or two)[9] about Cerridwen, who appears therein as a shapeshifting witch hell-bent on infanticide. It is said that Cerridwen gave birth to two children, a most beautiful daughter named Creirwy, and Afagddu, a son who was extraordinarily ugly. Being a perfectionist, Cerridwen sought to compensate for Afagddu's ugliness by cooking up a magic brew that would render him highly intelligent. This, she thought, would make him more acceptable and pleasing to her. So she found a recipe in a grimoire of Vergil of Toledo (the Roman poet Virgil, here transformed by medieval legend into an archetypal sorcerer), and boiled a cauldron full of inspiration and knowledge.

The brew required much tending; it needed to simmer for a year and a day. When the planetary hours were correct, Cerridwen gathered the magical herbs of the season and added them to the pot, which also had to be stirred constantly. A young lad called Little Gwion of Llanfair was put to this task. All year long he stirred the potion, and when the time was almost at an end, three drops of brew flew out of the cauldron, scalding Gwion's finger. He stuck his finger into his mouth to cool it off, and immediately received knowledge of the past, present, and future. He also saw into Cerridwen's plan to kill him when the magic brew was complete.

Gwion ran away, but Cerridwen pursued him, the guise of thoughtful and vigilant mother now set aside for the Bone Mother's mask of black, screaming hag. Gwion used the powers of the cauldron to change into a hare, but Cerridwen chased him in the form of a greyhound. He became a fish and dove into a river, but Cerridwen shifted into the shape of an otter. Gwion then became a bird and soared into the sky, but Cerridwen became a hawk and flew after him. Finally, in desperation, Gwion remained still on the floor of a barn, disguised in the shape of a grain of winnowed wheat. But Cerridwen changed into a black hen, scratched him with her feet, and ate him. Upon returning to her own form, she discovered that she was pregnant, and nine months later she bore Gwion as a child. He was the most beautiful baby boy she had ever seen and, since physical beauty was what she had really wanted to create in the first place, she could not bear to kill him. Instead, she tied him into a leather bag and threw him into the sea two days before May Day. He was found, given a new name, and embarked upon his own legendary career as Taliesin the bard, whose gift of poetry remains in the world to this day.

There are many modern forms of devouring one's children. Recently, there was a great deal of attention drawn to Susan Smith, the distraught mother who intended to kill herself and her two little boys by driving the family car into a lake. However, she only partially succeeded in bringing her death wish to fruition. At the last minute she had a change of heart; she saved herself and watched as the water closed over the top of the vehicle, her little ones still strapped inside. Seemingly in shock, she went to the police, claiming that a black man had stolen her car and kidnapped her children. A week or so passed. Susan held on to her story, crying her eyes out on national television for help in the nationwide search that was underway. Finally she broke down and admitted to the murders. Her reason for destroying her children? Her husband was abusive, her marriage was on the rocks, she was having an affair and couldn't handle the guilt. Something inside Susan snapped, something wild. Hurt, rage, fear, doubt, shame—a tidal wave of monstrous sensations swept away a family, a community, a country, the world. Susan may have driven the car that day, but there was a madwoman within her who stepped on the gas.

More often than not, such literal displays are (thank the gods) relegated to members of the animal kingdom, the occasional serial killer, and fairy tales—such as the story of Baba Yaga, the old wild hag of Slavic myth who was always looking for tasty little children to eat. However, there are other "motherly" but nefarious activities which may be just as damning to our psychological health as actual devourment is to our physical bodies.

Verbal, emotional, and physical abuse, abandonment, rejection, and disloyalty all play a role in damaging the child's vulnerable psyche. Perhaps the most insidious mother is the one who won't let go—who clings to her children as to a veritable lifeline, even after they have grown into young adulthood. This blights the process of separation from the mother which is essential to the maturation of the child's personality. For instance, Jung tells us that it is the mother who first receives from her son the projected image of the boy's own inner woman, his anima. In time, one hopes, the imprint of the boy's mother will dissolve gently, to be replaced by the true and unadulterated image of his own inner muse—which he will then proceed to project, madly, upon every wild Iseult who walks into his classroom or neighborhood! If the mother's image fails to dissolve, the boy will never be whole.

The result of the Terrible Mother's failure to let go is often a psychic trauma that affects the child throughout her or his formative years, and beyond, through indefinable dream images and shadowy memories filled with persistent childhood fantasies. When a daughter's fantasies relating to the Devouring Mother are particularly dark, it can diminish her resources in terms of self-identity, sexuality, and her own ability to embrace motherhood.

Victims of childhood trauma often feel tremendous shame, especially if the trauma has been sexual in nature. Then the sense of shame is doubled, for it leaves the adult feeling dirty and somehow less than human.[10] When a woman is sexually abused as a child, she is forced to enter into a very unpleasant portion of the Otherworld—the place where the Badbh's raven shrieks and the hag Baba Yaga hunts for meat—at a very early age. The little girl must face her demons, her shadow self, before she is ready to process the experience. This programs her primal, reptilian brain—responsible for all our automatic and hence natural functions—in a very negative way. When she grows into adulthood, she may be unable to release the past, which will descend upon her in dreamlike memory waves—monstrous, nebulous, and unbidden—which haunt her present existence and the lives of her children.

However, not all repetitive daydreams or nightmares of this nature indicate childhood sexual abuse. In fact, there currently exists an overwhelming number of reports concerning recollections of abuse, some of which appear to be false "memories," induced by therapists through artificial means such as hypnotic regression or guided mental imagery coupled with suggestion. Carl Sagan has expressed the notion that the common themes in dreams which appear to relate to this kind of abuse—i.e., being chased by monsters or wild animals, the sensation of falling—reflect the menaces common to our most ancient ancestors, thus suggesting that a form of genetic memory may be at work.[11]

Indeed, it is hard to imagine that certain drastic forms of trauma and abuse are "forgotten," only to resurface later on in vague and fearful recollections. If you break your leg, get kidnapped by strangers, or get burned in a fire, you are going to remember it. Why should it be less so when a parent forces sexual relations or physical and emotional torment on a small human body? Perhaps, in some cases, we really do "forget," because of our inability to believe that the very people deemed responsible for guarding and protecting us might actually be capable of causing us severe harm or even death. After all, babies are completely vulnerable and dependent creatures who have no choice but to trust the adults in charge. How awful when that fragile trust is violated and the child grows up trying to avoid being eaten by the "witch" or "warlock" who is also Mom or Dad.

Unfortunately, such patterns of abuse stretch far beyond childhood. Abandonment, rejection, disloyalty, and verbal or emotional abuse, like sexual abuse, can all limit or prevent an adult from achieving success in life. On the other hand, the fear of being left alone to die may also impel an individual to seek a high position or important career in the world. More often, however, such a person will embark on one career after another, only to abandon each one as she approaches the point of professional competence. Occasionally, suicidal or murderous fantasies involving the errant parent or adult will dominate one's life, for the anger experienced in the face of impending separation from the source of sustenance and nurturing has, by necessity, been repressed. Most likely there will also be great difficulty in expressing and handling normal feelings and emotions.

Seeking approval and winning the love of parents and others is often a primary defense against the fear of infanticide; sometimes this persistent hope of love is such an essential part of the child's innate defense mechanism that an elaborate system of self-deception is created, involving the distortion of both the child's and the parents' identities. It is theorized that the last outpost of this system of self-deception is the fantasy of being "not human."[12] This phenomenon may include feelings of invisibility, disappearance, dissolution, of being "not real," being a superhero, or being born on "the mother ship."

All women have a dual nature, and there is no such animal as a mother who is $99^{44}/_{100}\%$ pure—as the Ivory Soap Queen of commercial fame was purported to be, until it turned out she was also a porno queen! Today, at least, our "pop culture" of television sitcoms seems more inclined to admit to human ambivalence. How would you like to have television's Roseanne for a mom? Nagging, ridiculing, providing only brusque affection and loose meat (yum?)—at least she's there at home, tending her brood, albeit not so tenderly. Or how about Peg Bundy of *Married with Children,* television's favorite psycho mom? She's home, too—plopped on the couch in front of the tube while her daughter pleasures all and sundry, her son pleasures a plastic doll, and her husband pleasures himself with thoughts of suicide. These, of course, are caricatures, extreme examples. Most women tend to fall somewhere in between the good, the bad, the ugly, and the Terrible Mother.

When a woman feels empowered and is both physically and psychologically active in making her own life decisions, she is more likely to experience a sense of attunement with her body, especially during the intensity of labor. The more passive she is, the greater her difficulty in the birthing process is likely to be. In the latter case, the pangs of childbirth enable her to become a victim of fate rather than a responsible, capable, independent, and accepting participant in union with body, mind, emotions, and nature.[13]

It is also important that a woman feel uninhibited in her life, for this sense of free expression allows her to be open, both physically and mentally, to the birth of her child, and onward into childrearing. When she is able to express herself through her body, mind, and emotions, the new mother is less likely to impose her fears upon her child and thus perpetuate the Devouring Mother syndrome.[14]

The more a woman feels victimized by outside circumstances, the more likely she is to feel alienated from—and perhaps even hostile toward—her overall beingness. This is especially true if she has been pampered, spoiled, and over-protected.

Maybe this is what happened to Rhiannon. Her father, Heveydd the Old, was apparently a domineering old patriarch who tried to control important aspects of her life, such as her marriage. Pwyll and his entire court probably doted upon her as well, for after all she was a woman of faery, and inspired the sort of awe which that Otherworldly presence always creates. Rhiannon herself, being less of this world than of the great barrow mound of the unconscious, may have felt victimized by the painful and painfully human process of labor, and so experienced disharmony and conflicting emotions upon birthing her child. Of course, the myth speaks in its own terms, and not in the language of modern psychology. It simply recounts the aftermath of her experience, and leaves us to deduce the rest. If outside circumstances are a true reflection of our state of mind, our inner life, then we may well give ourselves pause to wonder exactly how Rhiannon internalized the process of giving birth to Pryderi, a child of this world.

So many monsters, so little time! We fear, we fantasize, we hope to be loved. If we are not loved, or if the love we attempt to give is not well received, we experience a sense of dread akin to the feeling of impending death. Metaphorically speaking, we are being summoned to the Otherworld to stand before the Death Goddess. Will she devour us, break down our flesh, suck out our life force, and leave us nothing save our marrowless bones? Shall we allow her to make ritual, reconstitute us, reawaken us, and make us whole? Or shall we accuse her of devouring us, her children, and thus hide behind our own denial, falsehood, and fear, like the women who attended Rhiannon?

The answer lies in the end of this most peculiar of tales.[15] Let us join Rhiannon at the horse block.

There was a man named Teyrnon Twryf Liant, lord of Gwent Is-Coed, and he was very good. In his stables he had a mare that was

the most beautiful horse in all his kingdom. Every year, upon the feast of Beltane, the mare would give birth, but never did Teyrnon and his wife get one of the foals. They found this very disturbing.

So when May Eve came again upon them, Teyrnon thought to learn what ill fate took away his colts. He stood watch that night, and lo, the mare cast forth a handsome, sturdy colt that immediately stood up in place. Teyrnon rose to inspect the colt and was stopped in his tracks by a great commotion coming from the black night. Suddenly a claw came through a window and grabbed the colt by the mane. Lightning quick, Teyrnon took his sword and cut the clawed arm off at the elbow. Again a great commotion, and then came a scream. Teyrnon pursued the sounds out into the darkness, but saw nothing. Remembering that he had left the door wide open, he rushed back inside to the colt he had saved and found there also an infant boy wrapped in brocaded silk. He brought the boy to his wife, who had no child of her own, and she welcomed him and called him Gwri Golden Hair, because his hair was the yellow of gold. He grew strong and smart and large for his age, and he was very fond of horses.

Meanwhile, Teyrnon and his wife heard news of Rhiannon and her penance. Noticing that Gwri Golden Hair so much resembled Pwyll, they decided to bring the boy to Arberth. They could see Rhiannon by the horse block upon their arrival. As they neared, Rhiannon said, "Lord, do not go any further of your own accord. I will carry each one of your party to the court upon my back, for I have killed my only son with my bare hands." But Teyrnon and his party kindly refused her offer and continued on their way.

They sat down in the hall to meat—Pwyll, Rhiannon, Teyrnon, his two companions and the boy. Finally, Teyrnon recounted his full adventure to the court, and, when he was through, no one denied that indeed Gwri was Pwyll's son.

"Between me and the gods," said Rhiannon, "I will be relieved of my care and anxiety if this is true."

At that moment, Rhiannon had named her son Pryderi,
which means "care" or "thought" in Welsh, for those were her first
words regarding him. He grew into the most gallant, handsome,
and best-skilled man in all the kingdoms, and ruled the seven
cantrevs of Dyved prosperously following Pwyll's death.

A clawed hand reaches out of the dark night on May Eve, perhaps to bring life, perhaps to bring death. The howling apparition that Teyrnon confronted in his barn may remind us of the Irish banshee, the spectral "woman of the hills" who comes howling out of the darkness and whose arrival portends death. The banshee, too, must have her claws, or at least talons, for she is often imaged as a bird of prey (usually a raven or crow, like Badbh or the Morrigan).

The identity of the mysterious nocturnal figure, then, should be clear. The Death Goddess who took Pryderi away finally gave him back, just as Cerridwen, after trying so hard to destroy Little Gwion, ended up giving birth to him again and sending him forth on May Day. The Bone Mother takes away, and the Bone Mother gives back again. But why?

Obviously, during her long ordeal at the horse post, Rhiannon faced the Terrible One. The Old Death Goddess is also a goddess of regeneration; new life arises out of the process of spiritual death. To undergo such a process, to come face to face with the Old One, empowers a woman. Our question, properly stated, is: When a woman—no longer a maiden but a mother—faces the Old Death Goddess on these terms, what kind of empowerment can she expect to gain?

If Rhiannon's story ever provided a solid answer to this question, that answer has been lost in the mists of time. But we do have a solution of sorts, one which comes to us from Rhiannon's Irish counterpart, Macha.

Not only is Macha an aspect of the Triple War Goddess, she herself is triple—for there are no less than three Machas in Irish myth. When we met her last, she wore the tormented mask of the sheela-na-gig, giving birth in pain, suffering, and loss. The second of the three Machas shows us an entirely different aspect of the Great Mother of All.

An Irish tale called "The Book of Invasions" records the mythological history of Ireland, seen as a wave of successive invasions by various peoples. The third "race" to occupy the island was that of Nemedh, who changed the shape of the land by creating four lakes and clearing twelve plains. One of these plains was called Ard Macha or "Macha's Plain," for Macha was the name of Nemedh's wife. Ard Macha—the present-day County of Armagh—is part of Ulster, where, in time, the fortress of Emain Macha was to be erected.

Macha, then, is part of the Irish landscape itself. She is, quite literally, Mother Earth. The old Celtic landscape is dotted with such tributes to the Earth Mother, the most famous being the so-called "Paps of Anu," twin hills in Kerry which are said to be named for the breasts of the Divine Mother called Danu or Anu. Some have theorized that the gigantic bulk of Silbury Hill, built by humans near Stonehenge on Salisbury Plain, is another such monument to the goddess of the land. The oldest megalithic tombs are comprised of an earthen or stone passage leading into a rounded chamber, and it has been argued that such structures symbolize the uterus and birth canal of the Divine Mother. The Neolithic villagers buried there were returning to the source of all life—a literal return to the great barrow mound of the unconscious. Such spiritual notions stretch back to the fifth millennium B.C., and thus are several thousand years older than the first appearance of the Celts in the British Isles. The Celtic invaders simply adopted a way of life which was too deeply ingrained to fade out.

The landscape as goddess finds its way into old Celtic poetry as well. A folkloric figure called the hag of Beare is credited with dropping stones out of her apron in County Meath to create cairns, with creating islands west of Kerry and mountains in Scotland, and with being the queen of the Limerick faery folk. She was young and old again seven times, so that all her husbands died and all her children gave birth to races and tribes. She was sometimes known as Bui, wife of Lugh, the god of kingship. Her home is in the great megalithic tomb of Knowth.[16]

In the early Middle Ages, an Irish monk with a fine sense of poetic nostalgia for the old Pagan days wrote a poem about her[17] which is sometimes regarded as the greatest single work of Gaelic literature:

The sea cringes away
from the shore
and leaves an ugly weed,
a corpse's hair.
Within me,
That desolate departing sea.

The Hag of Beare am I.
Beautiful once,
now all I know how to do is die.
I'll do it well.

Look how my skin
is stretched tight to the bone.
Where kings once kissed me,
now there's only pain.

I loved the wine
That tingled to my fingertips;
but now a cruel wind
burns salt into my lips.

The cowardly sea
slinks away from me.
Fear brings back the tide
that made me lie down by the side
of one who took me briefly for his bride.

The sea is waning, waning now.
Distantly it goes
and leaves me stranded here
where sea foam withers on deserted shores,

dry as my shrunken thighs,
as my tongue against cracked lips,
as my veins breaking through my hands.

To judge by the poem, the Earth Mother is in a bad way. We may well be reminded of Macha's terrible birth pains, the twisted face of the sheela-na-gig, or Rhiannon's lonesome penance by the horse post.

But why is the Earth Mother suffering, and is there a way for her to flower again?

Do you remember our tale of Gawain and the Loathly Lady? Here is yet another version of the same story.[18]

Long ago, the King of Ireland had five sons. The princes were forced to undergo a number of tests to determine which one should reign. They were all sent out hunting. They killed a boar and lit a fire. Then they were seized with a great thirst and went in search of water. Each one in turn came upon an old woman seated next to a well. The woman was hideous, with leprous skin, hair like a horse's mane, long green fingernails, and mossy green teeth like the huge fangs of an animal. (We know who she is—she's the Loathly Lady.)

The water in the well was fresh and cool, but the old woman would not allow the king's sons to drink from it unless they made love to her first. Three of the brothers fled in terror. One gave her a peck on the cheek and then fled in turn. Only the prince named Niall agreed to lie with the hideous hag. When he did so, the hag was transformed into the most beautiful woman anyone had ever seen. And she told Niall, "Lordship is mine, for I am Sovereignty." She named him High King and let him drink of the waters of the magic well.

The old hag, then, is a shape-changer of sorts; she is the Goddess of Sovereignty. But who may that be?

In ancient times, Irish kings took part in a ritual marriage with the spirit of the land. This earth spirit was perceived as the Goddess of Sovereignty. She was transformed through divine marriage from an old hag into a beautiful woman, as the earth itself is transformed from winter into spring through its marriage with the returning sun.

The king is emblematic of the sun. The sun is emblematic of the Self. As we know from the story of Gawain and the Loathly Lady, simply marrying "a man" (any man) isn't going to make a woman shed all her problems and turn radiant forevermore. But a divine marriage with the Inner Self just might do the trick.

Most scholars agree that, of the various tales in the *Mabinogion,* there is only one which can lay claim to being as old as the first four tales or "branches" (it may even be older). This is the story called Culhwch and Olwen,[19] in which one of King Arthur's knights, named Culhwch, seeks the hand of a maiden named Olwen. This Olwen, however, is guarded by a fierce giant, who sets Culhwch a number of impossible tasks to perform before he can win her. The final task is to hunt and slay a great wild boar, but for this task Culhwch will need the assistance of Mabon the hunter.

Mabon, however, is nowhere to be found, for he was stolen from his mother Modron when he was only three days old. Culhwch calls upon four of Arthur's heroes to search for Mabon; they question the oldest, wisest animals in the forest, but none have heard a word concerning Mabon, son of Modron. Only the ancient salmon possesses useful information, for he has heard a prisoner weeping and sighing behind a stone wall in a prison in Gloucester. The four knights go in search of this prisoner, who proves to be Mabon. They fight for his release, after which he leads the hunt against the great boar, so that Culhwch triumphs and wins Olwen at last.

This Mabon is a curious character, and, like Pryderi, he was stolen from his mother's bed shortly after birth. Does he hold the key to Rhiannon's redemption from her penance at the horse block?

Mabon's name means "Son, son of the Mother," and he was worshipped as a god in Pagan Celtic times. His mother, Modron, was known in Gaul as Matrona, who sometimes appeared in triple form as the Matronaes or Mothers, and thus may be taken as the archetypal Great Goddess herself. In Ireland, the god of love and joy was named Angus mac Og, or "Angus the Young Son," who is probably the same deity as Mabon. Angus was the son of the god Dagda and the goddess of the river Boyne, while Gaulish Matrona was the deity of the river we now call the Marne. The mother of Angus or Mabon is the Goddess of Sovereignty, spirit of the land.

In mythologies everywhere, the Divine Child is a symbol of the Self, that totality of being which, in Eastern religions, is called enlightenment. If we spin all these symbols around on the Silver Wheel, we may at last understand the full meaning of Rhiannon's story.

In giving birth, it is the Self, the totality of being, which Rhiannon has lost; it has been wrenched away from her by the Terrible Mother. Indeed, without facing the Old Death Goddess who lies within, a mother will become "terrible" herself—a Terrible Mother to match Blodeuwedd's Terrible Lover. When a woman faces the shadow of herself as hag and thus reunites with her real child, which is the inner Self, she makes a sacred marriage indeed. Only then may she rightly take her place as the Goddess of Sovereignty, spirit and caretaker of the land and the earth as well as of her own earthly children. When the Hag of Beare is made young again, when the Loathly Lady is transformed into the Goddess of Sovereignty, what manner of woman is she, and how does she express her empowerment?

We noted that there were three Machas. What of the third?

It is said that Macha was a great queen, bride of Red Hugh. This Hugh was one of three brothers, and it had been agreed that each of the three would rule Ireland in turn. But when Hugh died, Macha refused to surrender her power and sovereignty. Instead, she fought with and overcame Dithorba, the second brother, while marrying Kimbay, the third.

The five sons of Dithorba continued to hold out against her, and they fled into the wilderness. Macha followed them there, and one night she appeared to them as they were eating a wild boar around their campfire. She took on her most fearsome aspect, the Terrible War Goddess, bright red in color, with blazing eyes. Though the sons of Dithorba were struck with fear, they were also attracted to Macha's sinister beauty, and thus she was able to bind them up and carry them back to Ulster. There she unhooked her brooch—old Celtic brooches were made in the shape of wheels, crossed with long pins—and drew a circle on the ground with the pin (though one translation of Emain Macha gives the meaning "Twins of Macha," there is another translation, which is "Brooch of Macha"). This was to be the boundary of her new city, which the sons of Dithorba, laboring like slaves, built for her.

Here, then, we see a different Macha—regal and commanding, a proud wielder of power. As such, she may put us in mind of the most powerful woman in all Celtic myth, the great Irish Queen Maeve.

Maeve, Queen of Connacht, was an absolute ruler, both treacherous and grand, the sworn enemy of King Connor of Ulster and the Red Branch warriors. Her fortress was a "house of sky," for it had "seven circles" (the seven ancient planets) and "twelve windows" (the zodiac). As primordial goddess of the land, Maeve is responsible for the weather, and she brags that in her realm there are no clouds or thunder. When she urinates, three great rivers are created. She chose her husband Ailill because he was free of jealousy; Maeve boasted that she "had always one man in the shadow of another." Though she sent her warriors against the great Ulster hero Cuchulain, she also slept with him—and with Fergus Mac Roy, the old war chief of the Red Branch. Her grandiose appetites extended to wealth as well as sex—the cattle raid of Cooley, which formed the basis of Ireland's greatest Pagan epic, came about because Maeve and her husband Ailill had a bedtime disagreement over who was wealthier.[20]

Behind the archetype of the Mother lies the archetype of the Queen. Such is the empowerment given to women who, in motherhood and mature wisdom, embrace the Crone of Death and Rebirth.

Rhiannon came to our world from the Land of Faery. She adopted the customs and ways of Dyved as her own. She probably did this for her husband, Pwyll, as well as for the people of the land. Perhaps, in so doing, she put her Otherworldly powers aside for the time being. But she could not escape her inheritance from the great barrow mound of the unconscious. It came knocking on her door in a big way, to remind her: use it or lose it.

Though the tales in the *Mabinogion* are, as we have noted, garbled with centuries of Christian "revisions," we may nevertheless suspect that Rhiannon's decision to remain silent and perform her penance is an act of self-empowerment. She did not fall into contentious discourse with the six women who had lied against her, and in time she got her son back, thus exonerating herself and proving the women wrong. Her choice to be silent built a storehouse of power around her, for who knows what spells she may have muttered under her breath while waiting alone by the horse block.

Women have forgotten how to listen to their own wise counsel. They have become dependent on their mothers, aunts, sisters, best friends. Or, more and more, they depend on their therapists—who tell them that those same mothers, aunts, sisters, best friends, or anybody who ever brushed up against them at a bus stop are responsible for their organic weaknesses, depressions, and general hormonal malaise.

Throughout her life, a woman experiences many shifts in consciousness. The rhythms of her body continually change, and in a most perceptible way. She goes from the virginal state to puberty to defloration to pregnancy to delivery of a separate soul. She experiences the smaller rhythms of menstruation, weaving a cellular network which culminates in the greater rhythm of pregnancy, and finally, menopause. It has been said that because a woman's sexual power and desire often have to be repressed, she feels anger, which is then converted to depression.[21] However, a woman's anger is actually a message from the gods, letting her know she's alive. If a woman remains sharply aware of the changes in her body and willingly accepts the not-so-subtle nuances of her life cycle on a monthly basis, she can begin to recognize her own empowerment and thus re-establish her connection with the unseen. It is because women deny and/or ignore the Otherworldly forces that press in upon their lives from time to time that they experience difficulty with menstruation, childbirth, and menopause.

The truth is that by the time a woman makes a conscious choice toward motherhood, she had better have her act together, for she is about to receive the starring role as guidance counselor in the life of another soul. Unfortunately, modern society has (perhaps since the 1950s) provided us with little guidance. Who were our role models? If it was Mom, then lucky for you! However, many women of the baby-boomer generation have suffered from what current jargon calls a "dysfunctional family situation" in which the main theme was Father Knows Best—except that, as often as not, Father wasn't even there. Sad to say, Mother wasn't always there, either. So is it any wonder that, when our children look to us for guidance and we, in turn, look within, we come up empty?

Before we are able to tell ourselves what to do, we must know ourselves for who and what we really are. When a shamaness journeys to the Otherworld, she slips into the darker recesses of mind, heart, and soul in order to come up with the right answers. In traditional societies, this takes the form of specific exercises involving creative imagination, wherein one mentally enters a tree bole or a mouse dwelling and sees the power animals, elemental beings, particular plants and trees, and significant landscapes that play an important role in one's own process of self-discovery. By identifying with the special creatures and things pertinent to her personality, the shamaness can then understand her own motivations and desires.

In order to regain empowerment, it would seem necessary for a woman to return to her primal self. This does not necessarily mean that she must give up the dishwasher, food processor, or garlic press. It does mean that she must free herself from the sense of duty and obligation that goes along with the need to perform mundane, everyday tasks—at least long enough to let go of the idea of life as we know it in the "real" world. Wouldn't it be wonderful if a woman could be as uninhibited and childlike as the children to whom she gives birth?

When a woman, as mother, has faced the Old Death Goddess, she is transformed into a Goddess of Sovereignty who knows how to command, how to fight, how to exult in the wild joy of Nature and love. The sheela-na-gig is no longer a tormented woman, squatting in pain; she is a woman privileged to wear the wondrous mask of the Old Wild Hag, and her posture is neither more nor less than the one most suitable for giving birth in a natural way.

If a woman cannot properly manifest herself as a lover without facing the Death Goddess, neither can she manifest as Mother or Queen. The meaning behind the myths, then, is a constant one—the Silver Wheel spirals always back to the center, where the Old Crone herself lives in a wild splendor and deep, fearsome knowledge. Without these constant journeys back into the barrow mound wherein she dwells, we can do nothing.

Very well. Let us go and meet her.

Endnotes

1. Gantz, *Mabinogion,* 59-61.

2. J. E. Cirlot, *A Dictionary of Symbols* (New York: Philosophical Library, 1983), 218.

3. Anne Ross, *Pagan Celtic Britain* (London: Routledge & Kegan Paul, 1967).

4. Marija Gimbutas, *The Goddesses and Gods of Old Europe* (Berkeley and Los Angeles: University of California Press, 1982), 174-179.

5. Thomas Kinsella, translator, *The Tain* (Oxford: Oxford University Press, in association with The Dolmen Press, Dublin, 1979), 6-8.

6. Ross, *Pagan Celtic Britain.*

7. Shuttle and Redgrove, *The Wise Wound.*

8. Kenneth Johnson, *North Star Road* (St. Paul, MN: Llewellyn Publications, 1996).

9. See Patrick Ford, translator, *The Mabinogi* (Berkeley, University of California Press, 1977).

10. Lenore Terr, M.D., *Too Scared to Cry: Psychic Trauma in Childhood* (New York: Harper & Row, 1990), 228.

11. Ibid., 231.

12. Dorothy Bloch, *"So the Witch Won't Eat Me": Fantasy and the Child's Fear of Infanticide* (Boston: Houghton Mifflin, 1978), 228-229.

13. Gayle Peterson, *Birthing Normally: A Personal Growth Approach to Childhood* (Berkeley: Mindbody Press, 1984), 17.

14. Ibid., 18.

15. Gantz, *Mabinogion*, 61-65.

16. Proinsias MacCana, *Celtic Mythology* (London: Hamlyn, 1973).

17. "The Hag of Beare," rendering by Kenneth Johnson.

18. Cited in Caitlin Matthews, *Arthur and the Sovereignty of Britain: King and Goddess in the Mabinogion* (London: Arkana, 1989), 23-24.

19. Gantz, *Mabinogion*, 134-176.

20. Kinsella, *The Tain*, 52-54.

21. Shuttle and Redgrove, *The Wise Wound*, 306.

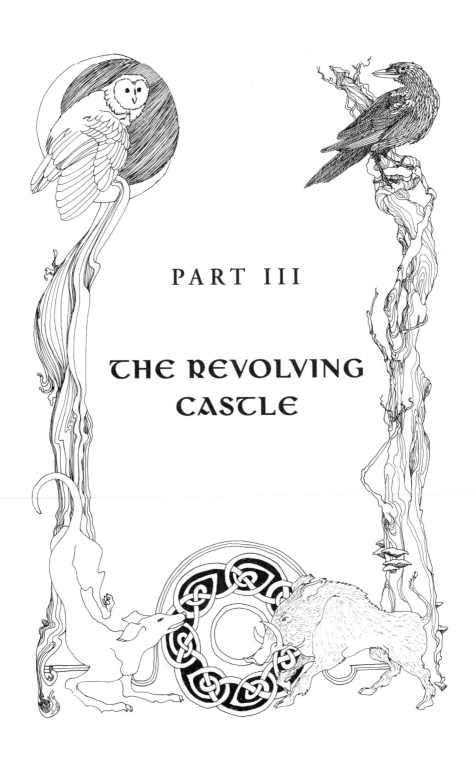

PART III

THE REVOLVING CASTLE

CHAPTER FIVE

She Who Would be Drowned

Creation rides on the wings of emotional gestation, a crested wave; a butterfly is born, a new sense of self emerges. With this renewal of spirit, the gift of self-forgiveness is granted and creativity is released....

Aﬧ︎ER YEARS AND YEARS HAD PASSED, there came an end to the life of Pwyll, Head of Annwn. His son Pryderi became the new ruler of Dyved and married Cigfa, daughter of Gwyn Gloyw. Pryderi bestowed his widowed mother Rhiannon upon the brother of the High King of Wales, and thus she became the wife of Manawydan, son of Llyr. The four of them—Rhiannon, Manawydan, Pryderi, and Cigfa—became inseparable companions.

One night the four of them stole away from a feast, and went to sit together on the barrow mound of Gorsedd Arberth—the mound from which Rhiannon had emerged so long ago, when she began her journey through the mortal world. As they sat there, the sky began to thunder and a thick mist came down, covering them with darkness. When the mist lifted again, all was bright, for it was day. And they looked about them with great amazement, for the whole land of Dyved lay before them and it was a wasteland. The buildings were empty, the farms deserted, the people vanished. Only they remained.

So the four of them took to roaming through the land.

One day, while Pryderi and Manawydan were out hunting, their dogs chased a wild boar into a mysterious castle. When the dogs did not come out, Pryderi went in after them, despite Manawydan's protests. Pryderi, like the dogs before him, failed to emerge, and Manawydan realized that the young ruler of Dyved had fallen under an enchantment. Sadly, he returned to Rhiannon and Cigfa alone.

Rhiannon stared at him in that way she had, and said, "Where are your friend and your dogs?"

Manawydan told Rhiannon the story. She replied, "A bad friend you have been and a good friend you have lost."

Rhiannon rode to the mysterious castle. The castle gate was open; Rhiannon entered. There she saw a fountain with marble stone all around it, and Pryderi, his hands frozen to a golden bowl and his feet stuck to the marble slab upon which he stood. He could not utter a sound.

"Alas, my lord," said Rhiannon, "what are you doing here?" She took hold of the bowl that held him fast and, as soon as she touched it, her hands became stuck there as well. Her feet stuck to the slab also, and she too was unable to speak. When night came, thunder pealed over the two of them, mother and son; mist fell around them, and the castle vanished.

Pryderi and Rhiannon vanished with it.

Thus Rhiannon, because of her son Pryderi and her husband Manawydan, had entered the Otherworld.[1]

When the mist lifted again, all was bright, for it was day. And they looked about them with great amazement...

We have compared a woman's journey, her spiritual path, to a wheel, circling into the depths of the Otherworld, the depths of one's being, and then spiraling back into the daylight world again. We may just as well compare it to the rising and falling of a wave.

She awakens as if from a dream, the winds of the gods moving her to a new place, just as the ocean winds move the water toward a new crest, a new cycle of motion. Her old way of being is disrupted by change, the impermanence of life, and she is then forced to let go. This act of release from the past can take a long time. It is a time of testing and can be very difficult. A woman needs quiet and solitude during this time to incubate her feelings.

Creation rides on the wings of emotional gestation, a crested wave; a butterfly is born, a new sense of self emerges. With this renewal of spirit, the gift of self-forgiveness is granted and creativity is released. During this time, a woman may also recover what has been lost. Following the flurry of creative activity, she may return to the shores of her former self, a wave crashing hard against the sand. She may be challenged by new tests, or she may lose her sense of direction for a time. She will be tempted to return to her old familiar patterns and foibles.[2]

But farther out to sea, the new wave is already rising.

The wave of Rhiannon's life has risen and fallen several times during our story. When she first emerged from Gorsedd Arberth, she was cresting, experiencing the fullness of creation, renewal, and emergence. She was beautiful, ripe with sunshine. When she returned to her father's kingdom she lay dormant for a time, gestating. Her wedding feast brought her a sense of reawakening. She was a bride, filled with hope for what the future might bring, a young woman ready to shapeshift her world. The charmingly deceptive Gwawl, encouraged by Pwyll's boyish pride, brought Rhiannon back again into the eye of the watery, emotional deep. The delay of her marriage forced her to let go of her dreams and feel her inner emptiness for a while longer. After Pwyll's return, she was filled with love and creativity once more.

Not only did Rhiannon lose her son at birth, she was accused of murdering him. At this time, she reached her lowest ebb, condemned to servitude and dark silence. With Pryderi's return, she emerged from the darkness older and wiser. Down she spiraled again when Pwyll's life came to an end; back into creativity and life she flew after her marriage to Manwaydan and her deep bonding with Pryderi and Cigfa.

Then, one day, she woke to find her kingdom blighted and empty. Her world had become a wasteland.

The theme of the wasteland is a major one in Celtic mythology, though it most often appears in tales associated with men. In a masculine context, the wasteland indicates that a man's primal soul is neglected and ailing; consequently his life is empty. When the high gods, the Tuatha de Danaan, sailed out of the north and into Ireland, they fought a battle with the Fomorians, a dark and brooding people who had occupied that land for centuries. They won the battle, but their king, Nuada, lost an arm in the process, and hence became unfit to rule—for in ancient Celtic society, no one with a physical imperfection could sit upon the throne of all the land. A Fomorian named Bres was allowed to reign as king, even though the Tuatha de Danaan had definitely established their presence. Metaphysically, it was a compromise between the light and the darkness in every human soul.

But Bres was not a proper king. He lacked generosity; his capital was not a very hospitable place. He served sour beer, and never any sweet mead. His sense of justice was warped as well. In time, the land began to cry out in protest. The cattle could no longer bear; the crops were blighted.

It took another battle between the Fomorians and the Tuatha de Danaan to re-establish the cosmic balance. Sometimes in real life, we can't simply heal our inner landscape by making war against our troubles. Consider the Grail Legend. The questing Grail knight—let us call him Perceval, which was one of his earliest names—happens upon a magical, mysterious castle. Within, he sees the Four Treasures of the Grail, symbolic of mystical wholeness, of enlightenment. Clearly, Perceval has entered the Otherworld—stumbling into it unaware, which is how most men get there.

Something is out of balance at the center of the Otherworld. The Fisher King who rules in the Grail Castle is sick, wounded with an incurable wound. Because of this, the Grail Kingdom is a wasteland.

We have explored the meaning of the wasteland and the Fisher King's wound in another book devoted to male myths.[3] Here, it is enough to note that the Fisher King symbolizes the primal, Pagan energy of earth and magic hidden within all men, and that men usually become aware that their inner Grail King is wounded somewhere around about the age of forty—what we call the "midlife crisis." If they are wise, men respond to the crisis by setting out on a Grail Quest meant to heal the inner king.

Having noted that, let us go on to note one more thing: It's different for women.

Because a woman is oriented toward *eros* rather than *logos,* she never entirely loses that sense of unity and oneness which constitutes the essential experience of the Otherworld. Seeking relationships, she is bonded with all things. Traveling in a circle, waxing and waning like the moon, she returns periodically to the deep heart of the Otherworld and drinks from the well of the collective unconscious. A man, by contrast, picks up his sword early in life—the sword, a symbol of *logos* or the mind, is good at cutting things up. It separates him from the Otherworld, the mystic Grail Castle of his childhood dreams. So he has to go stomping through the forest, traveling in a straight line, feeling more and more alien, until the Fisher King's wound is big and gaping and—just from the pain of it all—that straight line starts to bend, back to the Grail Castle.

Because a woman is always circling in and out of the Otherworld, she has many and various opportunities to drink from the well of the deep unconscious. But she may refuse to drink deeply, because she may be afraid of falling in. If she holds back long enough, skirting the rim of the deep well of her being, tightrope-walking along the edge of the Otherworld, then in time her wave will crash, and the life-giving water will bubble away, disappearing beneath the sand; the sea behind her will be calm and cold and gray, without any hint of a fresh wave rising.

Wasteland.

It doesn't need to be relegated to a midlife crisis. It can happen at any time. It can happen again and again. That's how it's different for women.

When a woman suppresses negative feelings on the upswing of her wave, she may experience them on the downswing. Whereas a man can simply withdraw into a place in which he can focus on his problems, a woman will hit an emotional rock bottom which renders her vulnerable and in need of more love and affection. A man may pull back, then venture in close; a woman moves from the threshold of herself into new life, undulating in her ability to love herself and others. A woman who has crested emotionally, then fallen, broken, on the sandy shore, may want (or sometimes need) someone to rescue her, to pick her up. Should she ignore the warning signs, should she not receive help, or should she deny herself the support she requires, she may be sucked headlong into the darker quarters of the Otherworld.

Different mythologies use different metaphors for that big gaping hole in the soul which we might call "the gateway to the Underworld." In Native American myth, you can simply crawl down a magic fox hole and there you are. In European myth, the Underworld entrance is often imagined as a great cave—in fact, certain caves in Greece were regarded as power spots because they were believed to be gateways to the realm of Hades and Persephone. But Rhiannon began her own journey by grasping a basin full of clear water. Why?

Throughout the mythologies of Celtic and Germanic peoples, the Well of Fate and Memory appears again and again. The Vikings wrote that the cosmos was a great yew tree, and that this World Tree had its roots in Hell and its branches in Heaven. In the middle of the trunk, a world—called Midgard or Middle Earth—lay surrounded by an ocean which, in turn, was encircled by a serpent. Shamans and magicians traveled *up* the World Tree when they went visiting the world of the gods.

But some shamans—especially women—specialized in making the journey *down* the World Tree into the dark recesses of Hell, to communicate with the spirits of the ancestors. When they reached the roots of the great World Tree, they found that those roots were fed by two primal wells—the Well of Memory, whose waters contained all magical or archetypal wisdom, and the Well of Fate, where the three sisters called the Norns spun the destiny of the cosmos as well as our individual destinies.

In Celtic myth, there was usually only one well. The World Tree of the Celts was typically a hazel tree rather than a yew, and it dropped hazel nuts into a pool which gave birth to five springs. In this pool swam an ancient salmon who fed upon the hazel nuts, and hence was the wisest of all creatures. Eat of the salmon or drink of the well, and one may gain all knowledge, all wisdom, all magic.

Where the Vikings imaged three Norns, the Celts often perceived one goddess. In various and sundry Irish tales, a hero who journeys to the Otherworld is met by a beautiful woman who presents him with a cup of shining liquid. If he drinks of it, he will never be the same again. This Lady of the Otherworld goes by many names, for she is not one goddess but all goddesses; in Ireland she was called Brigid, and though Christian legend has made her a saint who kept a "horn of plenty" (in the form of a magic pantry which was never empty, despite Brigid's habit of feeding hungry travelers), her original cornucopia was a Cauldron of Death and Rebirth.

Closer in time and place to Rhiannon's story is a tale called Owain, or the Countess of the Fountain, included in the *Mabinogion*.[4] The knight Owain becomes the champion for a countess who sits beside a magical fountain in an enchanted castle. Here again, we find the goddess seated by the primordial Well of Memory and Fate, deep in the Otherworld.

The myths of Celtic and Germanic peoples often send the female seeker diving down a well in order reach this Otherworld. Remember the story of Mother Hulda in Grimm's fairytales? A young girl with a cruel mother was spinning by the side of a well when she cut her finger (the evil mother made her spin until her fingers bled) and dropped the spindle in the well. She dove down to retrieve it, and found herself in a marvelous shining land—the old Pagan Otherworld, of course. There she met a woman named Mother Hulda, who seemed frightening at first on account of her oversized teeth.

Do Mother Hulda's grotesque choppers remind you of the Loathly Lady? They should, for Mother Hulda is but a recent variation on a most ancient theme—the Old Bone Mother, Goddess of Death and Rebirth.

A woman may have many and various experiences when she dives into the Otherworld well. The young maid in the Grimm tale was asked by Mother Hulda to do some household chores—chores which, being Otherworldly, had a profound effect in the upper world as well. When Mother Hulda shook out her bed covers, there were feathers in the house and snow in the world above. The girl did as she was asked with a good will, and hence was treated kindly by Mother Hulda, who sent her home in a shower of gold. But the girl's sister—lazier and somewhat malicious by nature—had a rather different experience. She thought she could get the gold just by diving into the well. Once she had arrived in the Otherworld, she too was asked by Mother Hulda to do a few chores around the place. But she shirked her work and sat idle (it failed to snow in the upper world and there wasn't enough snow-melt for next year's crops), so Mother Hulda sent her home dirty and covered with soot.

The moral of the story is: If we are pure in heart, we can descend into the great barrow mound of the collective unconscious and receive magical gifts from the Ancient One who dwells there. But if we sink into the well with all our imperfections on our heads, we are likely to have a miserable time. The metaphor of the Otherworld journey as a plunge into a well lives on in our collective imagery, and has served as one of the primary metaphors in a recent popular psychology book.[5] But so few of us are prepared to travel in those dark and misty realms that the book's author has made the well a metaphor for intense emotional despair.

Here are some of the warning signs that a woman may be emotionally en route to the darker canyons of the Otherworld:

Jealousy	Controlling behavior
Feelings of abandonment	Anger
Confusion	A mania for control
Excessive demands	Disapproval
Exhaustion	Frustration
Hopelessness	Insecurity
Lack of trust	A sense of being overwhelmed
Passivity	Feelings of rejection
Resentment	Withholding
Worry	All of the above (!)

To disregard these warning signs (especially if you are experiencing a fair number of them at once) is to risk entering a state akin to madness. Should this occur, any proffered help will vanish like the walls of the magical castle in which Rhiannon and Pryderi found themselves frozen. Night will fall and a peal of internal thunder will awaken you to a different place, one where your perception of reality will shift with the changing light. You will have crossed that fine line separating the shamaness from the madwoman, and you may become she whom you most feared to meet. Having taken such a dark and winding road to its Otherworldly ending, how shall we ever find our way back again?

Rhiannon, on her journey to the Otherworld, reached one solution, though there are others. Before you discover your own solutions, you must look more closely—and honestly—at the sharp rocks and dark holes that await you when you take the Otherworld road. Though we, the authors, may chronicle the experiences of various women, both mythical and real, who have traveled to the dark heart of the barrow mound, these can only serve as guidelines. In the end, you must make your own journey to the center of things, confront your own demons, and find your own road back.

Of course, you can always wait until life simply plunges you into the well, as it almost certainly will do. Even when an emotional crest has been reached (whether as a result of marriage, promotion, great sex, or whatever) and you have made contact with your own personal spirit of empowerment, there is no guarantee that you will retain the power you have won. In fact, it is most likely that what has risen will surely fall.

We must all prepare ourselves for that eventuality, for no woman can manifest herself as Sorceress or crone until she has made her passage through the Well of Memory and Fate. It is usually best to make that passage consciously, deliberately journeying to the Otherworld. Doing so will alleviate your fear of falling, flying, or both.

The following meditation will help you purify yourself for the Otherworld journey. It is important to perform this exercise prior to all journeys into the Otherworld.

Exercise 1: Purification Ritual

Sit in a comfortable chair. Loosen any restrictive clothing. Plant your feet solidly on the ground, and have your hands resting in your lap. Begin deep and rhythmic breathing. With each inhalation, breathe in the color blue. This color symbolizes the element of water. Envelop your body with this symbolic water until you are completely immersed in an oval of blue.

Now it is time to visualize the Great Goddess above you, life-sized and in living color. She is wearing a shimmering blue ankle-length gown and a long, gauzy blue veil that covers her head and face. A white, horned lunar crescent adorns her forehead, and she holds a silver chalice up to her heart with both hands. Her silver hair falls to her bare feet in undulating waves, creating a pool of silver stars that swirl in a vortex at her feet.

Mentally direct her into you; feel her spirit merge with yours; become her.

Notice that your robe flows from your lap like sparkling blue water. Begin to direct this water in a clockwise direction, swirling it around your body. After swirling the water clockwise seven times, quickly stop the motion.

Now think back to your past. Let your thoughts and emotions flow as you review your life experience. Sometimes particular instances will well up in your mind's eye. Calmly see them, bless them, let them go, and continue with the exercise. If your past moves swiftly by, with only brief images of important events, that's okay, too. Just bless your past and let it go.

Focus your attention on your poise, stillness, and balance. Again, notice the sparkling blue water flowing from the lap of your robe to gently swirl in a pool at your feet. Mentally direct this flow of water counterclockwise to the top of your Goddess selfhood. Continue directing it upward and let it spray like a fountain above your head. Let the water wash over you in streams of healing, purifying blue mist like a soft rain.

Experience the sensation of being cleansed and purified on all levels of your being. Thank the Great Goddess for assisting you and open your eyes. You are now ready to travel on to the next stage of the journey.

Exercise 11: The Otherworld Journey

This exercise will show you the way to the Otherworld. In order to make the journey, you will need a dark-colored scarf or mask to cover your eyes, a drum, and a friend to beat the drum.

If you have no one to assist you in this exercise or would rather perform it alone, a cassette recorder and a recording of shamanic drumming will do as well.

Find a quiet place where you can remain undisturbed for the duration of the exercise. Make certain that you are feeling calm and relaxed. Though not altogether necessary, it is helpful to abstain from all food and drink for at least four hours before beginning this exercise. Wear loose and comfortable clothing.

Darken the room you have chosen, and lie down flat on the floor. Have your friend with the drum sit in a far corner of the room, or have the cassette recorder with the drum tape ready to be played at your side. Your journey should take approximately ten minutes, so if you are using a cassette, have the tape set to correspond with the time.

Place the dark scarf over your eyes to further block out any light. Begin deep and rhythmic breathing, inhaling through your nose and exhaling through your mouth. Repeat this process four times. Next, relax your body, beginning with your toes and slowly working your way up to the top of your head. Be aware of any tension you are holding in your lower back, abdomen, and chest, and let it go. Allow the muscles in your jaw, mouth, and eyes to relax. When you feel completely calm and comfortable, allow yourself to contemplate the Otherworld journey you are about to take.

Now imagine an opening in the earth. It can be a cave tearing into the side of a rock cliff, a rent in the earth of a great barrow mound, a fox hole nestled beneath the roots of a tree. It might be a magical well in the forest, as in so many women's fairytales from all over Europe. Choose whichever image feels comfortable to you and one that you can visualize clearly. Take your time looking at the opening without making any attempt to go inside. Make sure to notice all its features and keep the details in mind. Is it near running water? Does it face east or west? What time of day is it here beside this hole or well? Are there any special rocks or plants marking the entrance to the Otherworld? Does a particular kind of animal live in or near the hole? And so on.

Now it is time for the drumming to begin. If a friend is helping you with this part of the exercise, inform him or her beforehand of the proper drumming technique. The drumbeats should be regular, with no variation in tempo. Your helper should stop drumming at the end of ten minutes, beating the drum clearly three times in order to let you know it is time to start making your way back. Immediately following, your helper should beat the drum very swiftly for a minute as a way of accompanying you during your return. Then he or she should once again beat the drum distinctly, three times, letting you know that the journey is over. If no one is assisting you in your journey, just wait until your picture of the Underworld entrance is nice and clear, then reach over and turn on the cassette recorder. The drumming on the tape should, of course, be timed for about ten minutes.

Imagine the opening you have selected and enter it. Walk into the great barrow mound or dive down the well like the girl in the Mother Hulda story. Whether walking or swimming, you will probably find yourself in the dark. Notice the manner of your descent. Are you moving down a steep incline at great speed, drifting slowly along a relatively straight passage, or swimming deeper and deeper into the depths of Fate and Memory? Does the passage bend sharply to the right or left? What do the walls of the passage look like? Are they ribbed or smooth? Perhaps you have moved through the passage so swiftly that you couldn't see any distinguishing features at all. This is all right, too. Sometimes you may run into a wall that seems to block your way through the passage. If this happens, try to find a way around or through it. If you find that you are completely blocked from moving further on, go back to the beginning of the passage and try again. What is important is that you remain relaxed throughout the journey, regardless of any obstacles you may encounter.

At some point, the drumming will stop and you will emerge from the passage into a natural landscape. Now it is time to explore this natural setting in detail. What are its features? Is it desert, forest, ocean, or mountains? Earthly or Otherworldly? What kind of stones, plants, animals, humans, or Otherworldly beings are there? Keep looking around for a few minutes, until your friend starts drumming again and calls you back, or until you yourself reach over and turn on the cassette recorder again.

Although you may have the urge, do not bring anything back with you. It is not yet time for that. Simply retrace your steps through the passageway or swim back through the water and follow the light back to your magical well in the forest, back to this world.

When you return, either tell your friend what happened during your journey or write it down in a magical journal.

Endnotes

1. Gantz, *Mabinogion,* 84-90.

2. Rev. Katherine DeGrow and Dr. Teal Willoughby, workshop material.

3. Johnson and Elsbeth, *The Grail Castle.*

4. Gantz, *Mabinogion,* 192-216.

5. John Gray, *Men are from Mars, Women are from Venus* (New York: Harper Collins, 1992), 112-113.

CHAPTER SIX

Arianrhod's Castle

The protean figure of Arianrhod stands at the center of a life-wheel which is both earthly and celestial, a complete metaphor or mandala symbolizing a woman's road of life....

THE SILVER WHEEL is a wheel of sky and a wheel of life. As a circle, endlessly revolving, it constitutes yet another image of woman's circular path—the path of the earth, of the seasons. In fact, the misty realm of the Otherworld itself—the great barrow mound wherein the Goddess of the Land awaits us—is sometimes called the Revolving Castle. The silver wheel, Arianrhod's Castle, also has its place in the sky, for the constellation we call Corona Borealis was known to the Pagan Welsh as Caer Arianrhod, while the zodiac itself was sometimes referred to as the Revolving Castle.

The protean figure of Arianrhod stands at the center of a life-wheel which is both earthly and celestial, a complete metaphor or mandala symbolizing a woman's road of life. But Arianrhod is a tricky and tempestuous character, for her story is one of feminine madness and wild destruction.

Is that wildness the force that stands at the center of the wheel? Or does the tempest at the heart of things also point out the way of redemption, the road from madness to majesty, the road to the sky?

Arianrhod was the daughter of Don. So much we are told by the *Mabinogion* itself. But who was Don? Nowhere in the surviving literature is she described with any clarity or in detail, but there are clues. In Irish myth, for instance, the high gods are called the Tuatha de Danaan, or Children of the Goddess Danu. In Wales, the heroines and heroes of the *Mabinogion*—who must once have been goddesses and gods—tend to be part of two distinct families, the Children of Don and the Children of Llyr. Was Don, then, a Welsh name for Danu, the great Goddess Mother of all living?

Probably so. Though the Greeks filled the sky above them with their gods and heroes by naming the constellations after various myths, we know very little about what the Celts thought about the sky. But we do know that the Welsh knew the Milky Way as Gwydion's Castle, and that Gwydion was one of the Children of Don. We know that the constellation we call the Corona Borealis was known to them as Arianrhod's Castle—and she too was one of the Children of Don. The star group we call Cassiopeia was "the Court of Don."

If Don was the great goddess mother of the Pagan Welsh, they also recognized a father god, a sky ruler who sat upon a throne above and beyond the world. This was Math, son of Mathonwy, and brother of Don. Arianrhod was Math's niece, then, and Gwydion's sister. The folktale which follows[1] must once have been a resounding myth about furious battles between the old goddesses and gods.

One day King Math the Ancient sought the counsel of Gwydion, son of Don, regarding what maiden he, Math, should take to wife. Gwydion was Arianrhod's brother and very fond of his sister. He recommended her to Math, thinking that she would enjoy being the wife of this powerful sorcerer who was also King of Gwynedd.

Proudly and with a hint of coquettishness, Arianrhod replied, "I know not but what I am."

She was fetched to him, and Math asked of her, "Are you a virgin?"

Proudly and with a hint of coquettishness, Arianrhod replied, "I know not but what I am."

So Math took up his magic wand, bent it, and asked Arianrhod to step over it. "If you are a virgin," he said, "I will know."

As she stepped over the magic wand, Arianrhod dropped a fine boy child with yellow hair.

The child began crying loudly, and Arianrhod, humiliated, bolted for the door, dropping yet another small object on the ground in the process. Before anyone could catch a glance at it, Gwydion wrapped it in silk and hid it inside a chest at the foot of his bed.

Math performed rites for the boy child and named him Dylan. At that moment Dylan ran for the sea and received the sea's nature. He swam away, never to be seen again.

Arianrhod's life changed forever the moment she reached the other side of Math's chamber door. We may wonder: Did she stand there for a moment, her chest heaving, listening for clues as to the fate of her reputation? More likely, she hightailed it back to Caer Arianrhod, her own castle and a safe refuge where she was in control of things, sheltered from the world—or at least from the judgment of Math. During her time there, she must have thought back, analyzing over and over again the circumstances surrounding her almost-marriage to the great king and magician.

She was a virgin yet not a virgin—she had been with child. How could this be? One tryst. Two. A god from the sea. Was she so rapt in the heady scent of brine that she lost her maidenhead to the offshore lands unaware? Did this mean she was now a mistress of the sea?

But never! No man or element had the power to possess her! She was the high priestess of her world, commanding elements, sorcerers, priestesses, and servants alike to do her bidding. Her body must follow suit. All was well and she was fine. The bent rod of Math meant nothing to her. She would get on with her life and put the whole embarrassing incident behind her—bury it far inside where it would never touch her again.

One wonders about the magical powers inherent in Math's wand; perhaps Arianrhod wondered also. A wand can be used to benefit others, but it may also be used as an instrument of punishment. Did Math intend to punish Arianrhod by causing her to jump over his wand? Or did he wish to alert her to her own inner depths, prodding her to recognize her own empowerment as a woman? Powerful implications surround the direction and intensity with which that instrument was used to ascertain Arianrhod's virtue, as well as its most obvious symbolism—that of the phallus, representing the perpetuation of life and the propagation of cosmic forces. Math's wand was indeed potent—it drew life from Arianrhod's womb. However, it had no power to create life. That feat, the secret formulation of cosmic substance, was Arianrhod's magic—a woman's power to gestate the spirit of the gods in the elemental depths of body and soul. Perhaps this is why it was so easy for Arianrhod to reject Math's role in bringing forth her issue. She and Math had not fashioned it together. Nor was the sea god, her lover, present to claim his offspring. She had made it herself—and she could unmake it, too.

Perhaps these feelings are encountered when a woman confronts the decision to have an abortion. Many women suffer tremendous emotional hardship following an often necessary decision to have an abortion, and do not need the added pressures of a judgmental, patriarchal, puritanical, fundamentalist society. The bottom line of the pro-choice argument can be seen on the popular bumper sticker which reads: "Against abortion? Don't have one."

Yet so many opposing viewpoints make it difficult to know what to do. Does human life begin at conception? Is the fetus a person? Should abortion be a woman's personal choice? Is it immoral? Can it be justified due to accidental pregnancy, congenital disorder, or rape?

Frank R. Zindler, a noted science writer, insists that "an acorn is not an oak tree," meaning that there exists the potential for the acorn to grow into a tree, just as there exists the potential for a fetus to grow into a fully functional human being, if the conditions are right. But the esoteric viewpoint differs, holding that life is no less the vehicle of a living soul simply because it is microscopic, especially after it has begun quickening in the womb. Furthermore, a union that bears fruit is one blessed by nature.[2] Therefore a woman must decide if she wishes to bear fruit of the body or of the spirit, and perhaps choose to use contraception rather than abortion if she only wishes the latter, thereby selecting the lesser of the two evils. Moreover, she must ask herself if she can live with her decision to have an abortion now and a year from now, something that Arianrhod should have done, but didn't.

We shall see, as we continue with the tale, that Math's part was indeed significant, though without conscious malice, and that perhaps Gwydion—trickster and shaman that he was—played a greater part in Arianrhod's descent into divine madness. However, we shall also see that Arianrhod's perceptions of herself were a little off from the beginning, and that, despite her talents and abilities, she continued to miss the point. The manner in which she was alerted to recognize her foibles, though shocking, life-changing, and certainly against her will, would perhaps have saved her in the end—had she been able to move past pride into willing acceptance, past the role of the victim to an exemplar of the feminine spirit. But she held fast to her rage, until it raised a great tempest in her life. Why?

Finally, we have reached that dark and thorny wood wherein most books concerning women's rites are in time led to wander: woman's war with the patriarchy. Until now, we have avoided the subject—in part because so many words have already been written, but also in part because of our belief that it is time women (and men) stopped searching outside themselves for the source of their spiritual, archetypal problems. Far better to let the rest of the world go its way, "an it harm none," while undertaking the great battle with the Self—which is more than enough warfare for most of us to tackle in a lifetime. For example, in the story of Branwen, we might well have railed against Mallolwch for imprisoning her loving soul within a cage, and condemned him as a blustering old patriarch. Instead, we have focused on how Branwen allowed herself to be imprisoned—or, more to the point, how modern women allow their emotional need for relationships to imprison them. Although it is no easy task to transmute the depths of your own soul, it is still a far easier task than changing the souls of the men in your life.

In the case of Arianrhod, we can no longer avoid the issue of woman's war with a patriarchal system, for Arianrhod, the Goddess of the Silver Wheel, is in open rebellion against the dominance of the male principle, represented by Math and Gwydion.

We remember Math and Gwydion from Chapter 3, for they figure prominently in the tale of Blodeuwedd. They were the meddling men who cheerfully fashioned a woman of flowers in hopes of creating a docile bed-mate for Llew Llaw Gyffes. They made the kind of woman they wanted—sweet and mindless, as mellow and fragrant as the daisies and daffodils from which she was sculpted. But these two lively lads learned what all men must someday learn: it doesn't work. Men can't image a woman as they would have her be—especially if their tastes run to the blithe, the blonde, and the brainless. The Old Bone Mother will come howling forth to greet them, and shake their hands with her own bony fingers—a greeting they just might not survive.

But we have told our tales in reverse, for Math and Gwydion grappled with Arianrhod some years before they fashioned Blodeuwedd out of the nearest wildflower patch. (After dealing with their respective niece and sister, you'd think they would have learned, but they didn't.) One cannot really expect them to do otherwise: after all, the Children of Don were sky gods. In most European mythologies (and in some that lie farther afield, like the Vedic), we find that there are two families of deities: one that represents the sky, and another that represents the earth, sea, and underworld. In Greek mythology, the celestial Olympians displace the earlier, earthier Titans. In Norse myth, the Aesir rule on high while the Vanir tend to the things of earth. It is hard to make such clear differentiations from the muddled surviving Celtic myths, but we have every reason to believe that the Children of Don (Math, Gwydion, and Arianrhod) were the gods of the sky, while the Children of Llyr (Pwyll, Pryderi, Rhiannon, Branwen, Bran, and Manawydan) were the older deities of earth and water. Taking this metaphor a little further, we may say that the sky gods more often represent "masculine" or "patriarchal" values, while the tellurian and oceanic deities have a stronger inheritance in the matrifocal Neolithic, the "old days."

Math and Gwydion, then, are the representatives of the celestial patriarchy. Math is a patriarch in the purest, most restricted sense of the word, for he is an old man, called the Ancient, and hence a father (Latin *pater,* from which we obtain our word "patriarch"). He rules. It's the rule of the father. Patriarchy, pure and simple.

Arianrhod, too, is of the starry race of sky gods. Like the Greek Athena, she is a daughter of the patriarchy. But unlike Athena, Arianrhod is in full rebellion against her would-be keepers.

To understand the nature of her struggle, let's get back to that intriguing (and dare we say?) little wand of Math's. There is a great similarity between Arianrhod's leap over the magic wand and an ancient custom usually associated with European gypsies or with rural Black Americans, known as "jumping over the broom."[3] The broom itself is, of course, commonly linked with witches—it is the vehicle of choice for traveling to and from the Sabbat. It can be made of birch, blackthorn twigs, broom, hazel, hawthorn, rowan, or willow. All these trees were sacred to the Druids, who had a special reverence for trees and who often invoked their indwelling spirits—something we still do every time we "knock on wood" for good luck and protection. These sacred trees, each bearing particular magical properties, also play a role in the old Welsh poem titled "Cad Goddeu" (The Battle of the Trees), which, according to Robert Graves, chronicles a battle between Arawn, King of Annwn, and the two sons of Don, Amathaon and Gwydion.[4] Here is a point worth remembering: before he married Rhiannon, Pwyll fought battles in the Otherworld on behalf of this same Arawn, while Don was Arianrhod's mother as well as that of Amathaon and Gwydion.

By Christians, heathens, and gypsies alike, the broom was regarded, when laid beneath one's pillow, as a source of protection against harmful spirits.[5] Let us not forget the simple but potent act of sweeping one's house clean of both literal and figurative impurities—nor let us forget that the broom is a symbol of household drudgery which, when used as an instrument of flight, is transformed into a metaphor for women's natural freedom. Finally, the original broom was, according to witchcraft and folklore scholar Margaret Murray, a "stalk of the broom plant with a tuft of leaves at the end." Murray also associated the broom with the "giving and blasting of fertility," an idea in keeping with beliefs about the broom plant itself.[6]

We may conclude that the broom, like Math's magic wand, is in some respects a fertility symbol, capable of producing animation, enterprise, energy, growth, and the renewal of life. Math holds the staff which symbolizes fertility, and he wants Arianrhod to jump over it. Incapable of producing fertility himself, he would seek to bend her fecundity and creativity to his will, to capture it somehow (Are you a virgin? Can I have it all?), and hold it within the power of his own symbolic will, the wand. It is her power and her creativity he wants and needs. Be a good girl, jump the hoop and give it all to me—that attitude and approach to matrimony left Math the Ancient holding his own.

Arianrhod has already placed herself in rebellion. She has already mated with a sea god—one in the older, more chthonic, "feminine" class of deities—and created Dylan, the child of the waves. Rather than submit herself to Math, she runs away, back to her castle by the sounding sea.

The wand, then, over which Arianrhod must jump is a symbol of fertility and creativity—and this is what is really at stake in the proposed union with Math. Creative energy, when not used constructively, can easily serve as a source of opposition and quarreling. This is what happened between Arianrhod and her brother Gwydion. Her initial rebellion against Math is about to blossom into a full-fledged battle with this archetypal trickster, shaman, and magician.

Arianrhod was responsible for three curses. The first occurred when Gwydion presented her with a beautiful, sturdy boy child about eight years after her fiasco with Math. Gwydion informed her that this was her offspring. Remember the small "something" that Arianrhod dropped by the door on her way out of Math's chamber—the small "something" that Gwydion hid in a chest by the foot of his bed? It was a male child, the twin brother to the sea-born Dylan. "It" grew up and needed a name. But Arianrhod was less than delighted when Gwydion presented her with her son. She wanted no way, no how, no part of it. She plunged into a white-hot fury and decreed that the child would never have a name lest she herself named him. And never would she do so, not in a thousand years. That was her first curse.

Gwydion, determined to have the child named, disguised himself and the boy as shoemakers. They made their way to Castle Arianrhod and announced themselves. When Arianrhod came to have shoes fitted to her feet, the child (who, by the way, was totally enamored of his mother) threw a stone at a bird and deftly hit it.

Arianrhod spoke: "The light-haired one hit it with a skillful hand."

And thus, unwittingly, she gave her son a name—Llew Llaw Gyffes, the Shining Skillful Hand. The same lad who would grow up to marry the maid of flowers.

As Gwydion gloated over the success of his ruse, Arianrhod swore her second curse: that Llew would never bear arms until she herself equipped him. That was something that, of course, she had no intention of doing. Gwydion stormed away, swearing that Llew would indeed bear arms, despite his mother's wickedness.

Again Gwydion tricked Arianrhod. Llew was reared until he could ride every horse and was perfect in every way. Once again Llew and Gwydion approached Caer Arianrhod, this time in the guise of two young men. They were welcomed into the castle, where they feasted and passed the night. Come morning, Gwydion summoned his powerful magic to make it appear that a great armada of ships was approaching to attack the castle. Arianrhod threw open her armory to prepare her retainers for a fight. Gwydion suggested that she give arms to him and his friend as well. She did so and thereby, unwittingly, granted arms to Llew.

Gwydion, once more overjoyed, suggested that Arianrhod might as well take the weapons back from her son, since there was no actual battle to be fought.

Enraged, Arianrhod swore her third curse on poor Llew: that he would never have a wife of the race that is now on the earth.

Seething at Arianrhod's cruelty to her son, Gwydion swore that Llew would indeed have a wife—that wife, as we know, was Blodeuwedd, the woman "made of flowers," created by the magic of Gwydion and Math and proving that, along with fathers, the sins of mothers, brothers, sisters, aunts, uncles, and third cousins twice removed are indeed visited upon the children.

We may disapprove of Arianrhod's wholesale rejection of her sons, and in her fierce refusal to acknowledge Llew we can already see that she is walking on the edge. Yet it is also possible to see Arianrhod as a woman driven to the brink of madness by a wild desire for freedom—like so many women in the old Celtic myths, she is possessed of a primal spirit, wedded only to the pounding sea, a spirit that allows no compromise or interference.

Arianrhod must always have had her shadow side—one that was exacerbated by the meddling of Gwydion and Math. Following the shattering of Arianrhod's self-delusions through the agency of Math's magic wand, one would expect that her brother Gwydion, who loved her, would leave her alone. Instead he demanded that she take full responsibility by acknowledging her child. One would think that he himself was the father, so dogged was he in forcing her acceptance. In fact, this idea is hinted at in Evangeline Walton's wonderful recreation of the old story,[7] as is the notion that Arianrhod's dark side may have turned darker still and that, following Llew's death at the hands of Blodeuwedd and Goronwy, she may have committed infanticide by murdering her son Dylan in order to rid herself of any trace of her past. In any event, it is possible to see Gwydion not as the archetypal magician—which is his usual role and his more appealing side—but simply as another representative of the patriarchy, trying to force Arianrhod to play by the rules, his rules.

Daughter of the sky gods, Arianrhod has rebelled against the stars themselves, seeking the wild primordial sea—which, like any elemental force, has slipped away from her, a tide running back from the shore. Math, her uncle, wants to own her sexual energy and judge her sexual freedom as well. Her brother Gwydion wants her to relinquish her aloneness, her magic freedom, and raise her son in the conventional way. The Children of Don have a few dysfunctional relationships in the family, to say the least.

How many of us have had relationships wherein the union falls far from the mark of our expectations—or just falls to pieces altogether? How many of us have misused our creative, poetic self for destructive purposes, thus feeding the madwoman within? Whether performing as actress, singer, cheerleader, beauty queen, model, teacher, student, therapist, mistress, or wife, many women have allowed themselves to be placed on a pedestal, the vehicle of another's inspiration and creativity. Thus a woman can easily be used and abused, physically, emotionally, mentally, and even spiritually, for gain or profit, by consciously or unconsciously sacrificing her talents and abilities. When her talents, abilities, and spirit have been used up, she is often rejected and abandoned. Her resentment in such a situation, if not rightly directed, may then be turned inward upon herself.[8]

Arianrhod was such a rejected lover, living in her castle of denial by the sea. But not for long. Ruined by Math, bereft of her sea-god lover, anguished by the loss of sons she had never really wanted, feeling forsaken by her brother (the deepest wound of all)—she hated them all so much that it was just as if she loved them. These thoughts and emotions must have ripped at her soul, shredding whatever vestige of sanity was left to her. Alone, abandoned, feeling abused and misused, despairing at the conflict between her role as priestess and her longing for love, angry at her fate, Arianrhod finally decided to take the ultimate revenge.

An old folktale,[9] preserved amongst the people of North Wales, tells of her fate. A certain rocky headland called Dinas Station was said to be the site of Caer Arianrhod, and it was inundated by the sea long ago on account of the evil of its inhabitants. In this story, Arianrhod had three sisters. They escaped because they were "righteous"—Gwennan flew to Bed Gwennan (Gwennan's Grave, presumably a Neolithic burial mound), Elan to Tydyn Elan (Elan's Holding), and Maelan to Rhos Maelan (Maelan's Moor), all of which were in the immediate vicinity of Dinas Station. Arianrhod, however, was drowned, and it was said that the walls of the castle could still be glimpsed beneath the waves when the tide was low. In Evangeline Walton's novel, Arianrhod chose magic as her way of getting even with the world, striking out one final time at Math and Gwydion, but succeeding only in bringing the waves down on her own head. A fitting end for the sorceress queen of Welsh myth.

Arianrhod's life had finally exploded in a tidal wave of emotion. The madwoman within her could no longer be contained. Rage may sometimes set a wounded woman free. Sometimes the anger and hurt is turned inward, resulting in physical disease or suicidal thoughts. Other times, rage is directed outward, hurting others in the process. Arianrhod responded to rage in a manner encompassing all of the above. Thus was set free the torrent that swept her out of life itself, into the literal Otherworld that one may reach only through death. In the world of Celtic myth, Arianrhod remains a great enigma, an archetype of righteous feminine rage. Queen of the sky and the pounding waves, she stands always alone, always rebellious, and sublimely mad.

Endnotes

1. Gantz, *Mabinogion,* 106-111.

2. Dion Fortune, *The Esoteric Philosophy of Love and Marriage* (New York: Samuel Weiser, Inc., 1977), 87-89.

3. Erica Jong, *Witches* (New York: Harry N. Abrams, 1981), 88.

4. Graves, *The White Goddess,* 30-37.

5. Charles Godfrey Leland, *Gypsy Sorcery and Fortune Telling* (New Hyde Park, NY: University Books, 1964), 136.

6. Margaret Murray, *The God of the Witches* (London, Oxford University Press, 1970), 92.

7. Evangeline Walton, *Island of the Mighty* (New York: Ballantine Books, 1975).

8. Linda Schierse Leonard, *Meeting the Madwoman* (New York: Bantam, 1993), 106-108.

9. John Rhys, *Celtic Folklore: Welsh and Manx,* 2 vols. (London: Wildwood House, 1983), Vol. I, 207-209.

CHAPTER SEVEN

Mystical Madness

At certain times in our lives, we open a door to some other reality, and there we see what we do not wish to see—a terrifying vision, a private apocalypse....

An old Irish tale, "The Destruction of Da Derga's Hostel,"[1] tells us how Conaire, King of Ireland, came to his end. He strove to be a good king, but carried with him a great burden. He was subject to many *geassa*, a Gaelic word meaning "taboos." Fate and destiny put King Conaire in the unfortunate position of being forced to break some of these taboos. As a result, his kingdom began to fall to pieces. Conaire and his knights ended up besieged by a fleet of sea raiders at an Otherworldly hostel kept by Da Derga, "the Red One." Things didn't look good.

Just after sunset, an old woman came toward the hostel. She was dressed in a gray, woolly mantle. Her mouth was on one side of her head and she had a beard that reached to her knees. She leaned her shoulder against the doorpost and cast an ominous eye on the warriors within.

Thinking that she must be a soothsayer, Conaire asked the old woman for her prophecy. She told him no one would escape from Da Derga's hostel except as carrion, borne away by the birds. Conaire was not terribly pleased with the augury; he asked the old woman her name.

Standing on one foot and holding up one hand, she sang out a whole list of names. Near the end of the list, she gave her real name, which was Badbh—like the Morrigan, a raven goddess who haunts the battlefield and whose approach heralds death (it is believed that the legend of the banshee is based on Badbh).

What she wanted, she said, was to come inside. This was another one of Conaire's taboos—he was forbidden to admit a lone woman after sunset. But Badbh insisted, and Badbh got her way.

The sea raiders sent forth one man to spy on Da Derga's hostel. He peeked in through the many magical doors of the place, and he saw many things—mostly Conaire's warriors. But he also saw Badbh.

"I saw three," he reported. "They were naked, on the ridge-pole of the house. Jets of blood poured through them, and the ropes of their slaughter hung round their necks."

"I know those three," said another of the raiders. "They bode doom, and they are the three who are slaughtered every time."

The raiders surged forth from their ships. They destroyed Da Derga's hostel and all the warriors in it. So Conaire came to his end.

Though this story is primarily concerned with men rather than women, the experience it describes is universal. At certain times in our lives, we open a door to some other reality, and there we see what we do not wish to see—a terrifying vision, a private apocalypse, three mad crones or ravens, covered with blood and naked save for the hanged man's rope.

We may wonder if the Great Goddess has a screw loose. If the Revolving Castle is but another name for the great cycling round of death and rebirth that moves all worlds, if Arianrhod may be taken as a symbol of the primal energy that lies at the heart of the great barrow mound of the unconscious, then her story seems to prove only that there is a wild raving madwoman beneath the love and light that shines (so we are told) on a woman's surface. Open the door and there she is—dancing, howling, her fangs dripping with blood.

Different mythologies use different metaphors for that big gaping hole in the soul which we might call "the gateway to the Underworld." In Native American myth, you can simply crawl down a magic fox hole and there you are.

In India, where the "terrible goddesses" such as Kali are still worshipped, it is said that these fierce manifestations of the feminine are helpful in "slaying our illusions." But what illusions are these?

We all build up many illusions about ourselves. We may see ourselves as free and independent, while those around us see us as clinging and whiny; perhaps we think of ourselves as generous to a fault, while those who know us better may regard us as the ultimate tightwads. In any event, we have constructed an illusory self-image, one which ignores or denies the existence of the darker, seedier aspects of our personalities. In time, these rejected components of our souls take on a psychic life all their own, and create a kind of reverse image of our ordinary selves; in Jungian psychology, this alter ego is called the Shadow.[2]

We may look into the mirror of everyday life and, like Snow White's stepmother, see only the "fairest of them all." In time, however, a greater reality shall surely take us in hand—and from the earlier chapters of this book, we know that it will lead us into the great barrow mound of the unconscious. There, we will look into a darker, less merciful mirror, and, again like Snow White's stepmother in the fairytale, we shall see the wild hag shrieking in our faces once more. We have seen our own Shadow. She isn't nice, but she is necessary. Goddesses such as Kali or Badbh reveal to us these hidden aspects of ourselves, slaying the illusions of "the fairest of them all." Sometimes, when our illusions crumble, so do our minds.

All women (indeed, all people) have the capacity for insanity deep inside them. If a woman allows herself to plummet too deep into her well, the eye of her emotional depths, then she may drown before she gets out again.

Suspended o'er the gaping chasm,
Eye of the ocean deep
Wherein demise looms sweet,
O, but that grey escape, an open door
To nothingness!
Such bliss and refuge
For one fallen to self-condemnation,
Worthy initiate for the deluge,
She who would be drowned
Or taken by the sky.[3]

We have already listed (in Chapter 5) several warning signs that may herald a meeting with the madwoman, the shadow side of your personality. If you are fortunate, you will be consciously aware of these mood swings and generic shifts of temperament; but what if you have emotionally checked out and, without quite knowing it, crossed the fine silvery thread that separates magic from madness?

Madness can take many different forms. A person can be a little off or a whole lot off, as mental imbalance can range from simple irratibility and forgetfulness to full-on lunacy. In some people, signs of disturbance appear only occasionally, while others display bizarre, unwarranted behavior all the time. One who is pleasantly cracked will generally be left alone, for society tends to forgive, ignore, or even protect the harmless eccentric who believes that space aliens have landed on Earth specifically to attack her nose. However, if madness begins to show itself in ways that are considered a threat to others or to oneself, more drastic measures may be taken.

Of course, it is not our intention to make light of those who suffer from mental illness. It is very sad to watch a viable, loving human being deteriorate into a helpless, mean-spirited stranger. But it happens sometimes, whether people are "just born that way" or whether they develop the tendency during their lifetime. It has been statistically shown that many artists, writers, and poets (who frequently delve into the Otherworld) are prone to bouts of madness.[4] Much as we may want to believe that madness only affects others, the truth is that we are all disposed toward it, whether by accident or when confronted by a quantity of grief sufficient to make us lose our balance. This is especially true if we are already prone to walking on the edge of the cosmic well.

Why should we wish to dance on the tightrope of chaos in the first place? What would impel us to do so?

One theory holds that mental imbalance is organic in nature. According to this notion, all mental disorders derive from physical changes in or damage to the body. Brain damage occurring before, during, or after birth, a stroke later in life, diseases such as encephalitis or AIDS, vitamin deficiency conditions, a blow to the head, and drug or alcohol abuse may all result in such disturbance. Since this form of mental "dis-ease" is physical in origin, perhaps it should not be classified as mental at all.

The latest findings in the field of psychological research suggest that mental imbalance is biochemical, meaning that an insufficient amount of certain chemicals in the brain may lead to various forms of mental aberration. This idea is supported by the fact that certain medications, vitamins, and amino acids seem to alleviate symptoms.

Heredity, genetics, and parent-child interaction also play an important role in our mental health, for it is frequently discovered that a parent or blood relation of someone suffering from mental imbalance also displays the characteristics associated with mental/emotional instability.

Abnormal brainwave activity over the temporal lobe (the lower side of each half of the cerebrum, the main mass of the brain) also suggests possible dysfunction, as do unusually high levels of certain pituitary hormones that stimulate and control growth, metabolism, and the sexual organs as well as many other functions of the body. These last contributing factors are most interesting because these areas of the brain and endocrine system are precisely those affected when a shaman or shamaness enters a trance state. We shall have more to say about this a little later on. But for now, let us ask ourselves: Exactly what happens when we lean too far over the edge of the well while looking down into the magic mirror? Just what goes on when we fall in and lose ourselves to the dark side of Luna, becoming "moon-struck"?

As most people know, words like "lunacy" and "lunatic" find their origin in the Latin *luna,* signifying the moon. Though the moon, in its positive or waxing aspect, may symbolize the nurturing power of the Great Mother, it is also, as Shakespeare called it, "inconstant," emotionally treacherous, and, in its waning phase, a symbol of the Dark Goddess, she whom we have feared to meet. To be a lunatic is to be immersed in the nightmarish channels of the mind, to live for the dreamlike images of a false reality, to turn our attention to the woman on the face of the moon or to the side of the moon that we cannot see.

And from this chasm, with ceaseless turmoil seething,
As if this earth in fast thick pants were breathing,
A mighty fountain momently was forced.[5]

As almost all Pagan symbolism makes clear, and as Carl Jung has confirmed from a psychological perspective, the moon represents the unconscious aspect of mind. When we dwell too heavily upon the unconscious, we become creatures of conflicted instinctual awareness; hence our lives may come to a standstill while the inner battle between instinct and logic rages on. We may be blind amid the dangers of reality and our own desire nature. The body attacks the spirit and the spirit is bound by the body—consequently, we experience obstacles and pain. The psychological term for this decidedly uncomfortable state of being, and one which most of us have experienced at one time or another, is repression.

When we are repressed, we refuse to allow new ideas to enter into consciousness. However, these ideas are not forgotten just because we have refused to accept them. They have to go somewhere. So we repress them into our subconscious memory, in a futile attempt to prevent that which is out of harmony with our present sense of order, or that which is primal and instinctual in nature, from intruding on our hard-won shell of confidence and self-esteem. Basically, we repress into the unconscious all that we find repulsive within ourselves, and that somehow reminds us of some long-forgotten aspect of the instinctual or primal self—most of which has been literally or figuratively beaten out of us by our parents, our guardians, the dictates of society, or any combination thereof.

We must remember that the primitive self is a sleeping dragon. If you force the mind to ignore the round peg simply because you believe that the hole in your head is square, the dragon will wake up one day when someone or something has disturbed a jewel from the hoard of treasures hidden in the secret cave of the unconscious. When the sleeping dragon awakes, all hell breaks loose.

Emotions arise from instinct, and instincts impel us to take action to fulfill our desires. When we are unable to fulfill our desires in waking consciousness, our minds will often resort to dreams and fantasy images in which we can be whoever we wish to be and have our needs met without obstruction. In dreams, everything is passing and ephemeral. Nothing is permanent. Sometimes dreams are seductive; sometimes dreams may be realized. Often, however, dreams are just flights of fancy, as if the nature spirits have come with their faery favors to help us, guide us, or mislead us.

Dreams and fantasy images are often fostered by past memories; hence the primal, natural self is able to express its most basic desires in raw, uncivilized, elemental form while in the dream state. Consequently, many dreams give us insights into parts of ourselves that are hidden from our awareness during waking consciousness. If we are healthy of mind, we may be able to put our dream visions to good use during the course of the day, although some dreams hold much more promise than fulfillment and will never be made manifest in physical reality. If we are not so healthy of mind, our dreams may express all the desires that are vested in our hidden complexes; yet we may strive to live out our delusions, even though they have no worldly substance to back them up.

Nevertheless, our dream castles are real on the subjective level of mind, and the imbalance produced by an unfulfilled desire can be healed when the foundation of our hopes and wishes is honestly assessed. If the logical mind chooses to tunnel deeper into the unconscious rather than turn back to the entrance—which leads to the light of daily reality—we may enter into the state of pathological forgetfulness called dissociation. This differs from ordinary forgetfulness, which is what happens when we simply "space it out" because we're not that interested in whatever-it-is in the first place. An idea that becomes dissociated is emotionally charged, repressed into the unconscious, and then returns to life with a power all its own, often when we least expect it.

Today the common buzz word used to describe this condition is denial. When we refuse to look at the ideas that upset us, when we are unable to take responsibility, to forgive and love ourselves and others, then our dissociated complexes eventually diffuse the energy available to our logical minds. We are reduced to living with the impulses of violent and chaotic needs, but with no way to formulate them into those productive channels of desire that lead to the satisfaction of real life experience. Then we are left with nothing but an empty void where our souls used to be, without the will, knowledge, silent mental space, or empowerment to fill it.

Dissociation or denial cannot occur if we are honest with ourselves. Although it is not normal, denial is common, even rampant, in our society—a learned, crazy-making behavior.

What if we are afraid to look? What if we cannot see or refuse to deal with our shortcomings and limitations?

Well, then, in that case we shall be primed to take the plunge into the well in earnest. We shall be about to enter altogether into the wonderful world of madness.

How do you know if this is happening to you?

It may become increasingly difficult, or next to impossible, to deal with the ordinary stresses of daily life. Perhaps the body/mind connection grows disordered or disturbed. Your friends begin to abandon you, or you develop chronic symptoms of illness without any apparent physical cause. Maybe you forget to perform the simplest tasks, or attempt to mask your problems with drugs, alcohol, or sex. Perhaps you become obsessed, preoccupied, filled with anger. Maybe you're ready to pluck out your eyebrows, pierce your forehead, shave your head, and dye your scalp green. (Okay, some of this may be part of the common trend these days, but that doesn't necessarily mean it's common for you.)

Perhaps the most widespread form of madness afflicting women is neurosis. The neurotic woman is usually an unhappy person. She can be extremely anxious without any apparent cause, feel guilty, depressed, and irrational for no reason, and have difficulty coping with the simplest routines of daily life. Again, denial is at the root of her problem, as she will devise elaborate ways to protect herself against her fears, the sources of which are usually vague and amorphous. The result is emotional exhaustion with little relief from inner turmoil. Worst of all, perhaps, is the fact that the neurotic woman blames herself for everything, even occurrences beyond her control. She is an expert at self-denigration. Not only does she try to convince everyone around her that she has done wrong, she continues fervently to believe that it's all true, thus perpetuating the cycle of neuroses.

Because she was once told to express her feelings ("There, there now. It's okay for little girls to cry"), and later to repress them ("Be quiet, you *@#! Can't you see I'm watching the *#! ballgame?!"), the neurotic woman is likely to suffer from anxiety. The typical anxiety attack may include feeling a loss of control, difficulty in breathing, racing heart or palpitations, nausea, headache, nightmares and insomnia, blurred vision, confusion, and unwarranted rushes of fear. Add uncertainty to the list and a full-blown panic attack may ensue, in which the victim is replete with feelings that she is not in her body, fear that she is dying, and feelings that she is going insane.

Since anxiety leads to fear and panic, phobia may not be too far behind. A phobia is a strong, persistent, irrational fear of an object or situation. It may be a signal that something is wrong within a relationship with the self or others. Flying, germs, churches, doctors, lawyers, snakes, and poverty are just a few of the types of fears to which one may respond in an irrational way (though, on second thought, fear of churches, doctors, and lawyers may not be altogether irrational).

Two other forms of anxiety that affect younger neurotic women are anorexia nervosa (self-starvation) and bulimia (binge-eating and purging). Both disorders find their roots in low self-esteem and a fundamental distaste for one's own body and identity.

Obessive-compulsive neuroses surround a woman who performs inappropriate actions against her wishes (compulsion) or who has repeated or uncontrolled thoughts (obsession). Ritual actions, such as certain forms of magical thinking to deal with and alleviate fears, fall into this category also. Jung believed that neuroses stem from an attempt to solve today's problems using primitive methods—in other words, there is a gap between the dictates of the collective unconscious and the effective solution of our day-to-day problems.

Depression, with its accompanying bouts of sadness, apathy, and unresponsiveness, is yet another way in which the neurotic woman masks her problems. Unfortunately, although the feelings may come and go, they tend to remain over time.

Though neurosis may be the most common form of mental illness among contemporary women, it isn't the only one, nor is it the most intense. That dubious honor must go to psychosis.

Psychosis is more severe than neurosis. The psychotic woman will display a strikingly different set of perceptions from ordinary people, and a loss of contact with reality. Psychotic delusions are strongly held thoughts that have absolutely no basis in fact. The psychotic woman will believe that others are talking about her when they are actually discussing something quite different (a condition that is technically called "psychotic reference"), or think that people are after her for no particular reason (persecution); she typically sees herself as being above or better than everyone else (grandeur).

Psychotic hallucinations may include sensory experiences that, like the stream of a psychotic's thoughts, have no basis in fact. Usually these fictitious imaginings will include a series of disordered ideas and emotions, including distraction, poor discrimination, and an obsessive attention to irrelevant details.

A psychotically depressed woman will harbor gloomy thoughts, hopelessness, withdrawal, exhaustion, and despair. In manic-depressive psychosis, these periods of deep sadness and lethargy alternate with mania, elation, and activity.

Schizophrenia is the most widespread and serious psychosis. The schizophrenic experience is not unlike the proverbial bad acid trip; withdrawal, loss of interest in the outside world, hearing voices, and extreme paranoia combined with a total breakdown of the personality will often characterize a schizophrenic episode.

Finally, as if the above-mentioned imbalances weren't enough, there is Borderline Personality Disorder (BPD), a little-known and thoroughly misunderstood mental/emotional imbalance affecting an estimated ten million people in America today. It is expressed in violent mood swings, a shaky sense of identity, oversensitivity to real or imagined rejection, brief and stormy love relationships, intense depression, eating disorders, drug and/or alcohol abuse, self-destructive tendencies, and fear of being left alone.

Are these, then, the mystic experiences that are likely to confront us when we finally take the spiral path allotted to all women and leap (or fall) into the great cosmic well?

In one sense, yes. But before we begin to despair over the necessity of traversing, at various times in our lives, the Revolving Castle, let us remember that the perspective of modern psychology may sometimes be one-sided. For as the story of Mother Hulda shows, the plunge into the well may bring ecstasy as well as despair.

In a tale more ancient than any of our Celtic myths,[6] the Babylonian goddess Ishtar descended into the Underworld in search of her lover Tammuz (yes, it was a relationship that plunged her into the well). Like all women who make that fearful journey, she had to give up her self, her identity, her sense of who she was. Since she was the Goddess of Love, that meant being stripped of her fine clothes and her beautiful jewelry, until she ended up naked in front of the Old Death Mother (who, in this story, comes complete with leeches in her hair) and was hung on a meat hook in the darkest part of hell. But when, at last, Ishtar was released to return to the upper world, she was no longer merely the Goddess of Love: she had become the Queen of Heaven. Her journey into despair ended in a kind of ecstatic wisdom.

What does this mean to the contemporary woman? Don't resist the descent into the well. It is not necessarily a bad thing. Try to plunge with your heart simple and whole, like the girl in the Mother Hulda story. Then, perhaps, you will behold the kindlier face of that Old Life-and-Death Mother, she whom you feared to meet.

She is, as we have seen, incredibly old. The spectral lady in white, the banshee who heralds the death of something useless and outmoded within all of us, is a descendant of the "stiff white lady" of Neolithic times—an icon that dates back to about 6000 B.C. This archaic goddess is but the descendant of another, older deity—the goddess of Paleolithic shamanism who raises us up from spiritual death by singing over our bones.[7] She dwells within the earth itself—whether we see that "earth" as the world at large, or the temple of our own bodies.

As such, she is a force of Nature—anyone who has ever stood outdoors during a raging thunderstorm knows that Nature is an absolute, a force, a power, an energy that knows neither good nor evil—a force that simply is.

Throughout human history—and probably as long ago as the Ice Age—certain individuals have chosen, of their own free will, to dive into the Well of Memory and Fate and traverse the dark corners of the great barrow mound of the unconscious. Such individuals are called shamans (in the present case we shall say "shamanesses" rather than using the more technical feminine plural, which is "shamankas"), a Siberian word that describes a specialist in the techniques of spiritual ecstasy.[8]

Shamanism is universal; though the word makes most of us think of Native American tribal magic, the shaman's techniques are practiced all over the planet. The shaman or shamaness, with the help of a totem animal (whose form the shamaness may sometimes adopt), travels to the world of the gods or the ancestors in order to seek wisdom there. This journey is sometimes induced by the use of psychotropic substances, though more often it is simply an astral experience brought on by the innate talents or specialized training of the practitioner herself.

The actual content of the journey varies from culture to culture, and even from individual to individual. Native American shamans, for example, crawl down a magic foxhole or through a rift in the sky in order to reach the Otherworld, while many European shamans climbed up the trunk of a great tree that linked the three worlds of gods, mortals, and the dead.

While many Pagan European shamans climbed up the World Tree to "the land of the gods," many also climbed down to the world of the ancestors, that great community of all the souls and spirits who have come before us and whose collective wisdom still guides us in the form of myths, dreams, and archetypes. There is a great deal of anthropological evidence to indicate that it was more typically the women or shamanesses who specialized in the downward journey.

Among the Pagan Norse, women had their own special shamanic rites, called *seidr*, dedicated to the goddess Freya, who ruled fertility, sexuality, and magic, and whose totem animal was the cat. An old Norse saga[9] describes such a shamaness, her blue mantle studded with gems, her head covered with a black lambskin hood lined with white cat fur, and her gloves made of catskin as well. She carried a staff that, like her mantle, was studded with magic stones, and she wore a pouch of runes at her belt. A platform was erected for her with a cushion of hen's feathers on top. While the local women chanted magical songs, the shamaness seated herself atop the platform, fell into a trance, and journeyed to the Otherworld. In such an altered state, she spoke to the people, prophesying their fates and dispensing wisdom from the world of the gods.

Shamanic practices persisted in Europe long after Christianity arrived, and frequently made their appearance in the records of the witch trials—the witches, in fact, were the village shamanesses of medieval Europe. They left their bodies, traveling up a chimney or broomstick as if climbing the World Tree. Sometimes they traveled in the shape of animals—especially cats, which were sacred to Freya. In the course of their astral journeys, they consorted with "elves" or with "the Wild Hunt"—in short, with the wandering spirits of their ancestors. They brought back Otherworldly lore such as herbal cures, divinatory practices, prophetic utterances, and so on.[10]

In 1662, the Scottish witch Isobel Gowdie testified[11] that she often left her body and, in the shape of a raven or a hare, traveled in Otherworldly realms. One night she swooped down to an old barrow mound, which opened before her to reveal the world of the faery folk. Inside the mound, she met the King and Queen of Elfland, the queen garbed in brown and white, the king "well favored and broad faced." After participating in a faery feast, Isobel took to the air again, shooting elvish arrows with the younger folk from the Downy Hills.

It is clear that Isobel Gowdie had gone traveling in the old Celtic Otherworld, and, like a true shamaness, had journeyed in the spirit to the heart of the great barrow mound of the soul. There she met not only the Queen of the Elves, but the king as well, of whom we shall have more to say in the next chapter.

For the moment, however, let us take a closer look at the Queen of the Elves. Who is she? The folklore of the British Isles assures us that she dwells inside the barrow mounds, where she and her elvish companions are engaged in an eternal, magical feast. On special nights, notably Halloween, she emerges from the barrow mound. Mounted on horseback, she gallops through the woods followed by the "faery troop," likewise mounted. When the faeries visit mortal houses, they seek meat and drink, for they are hungry when they come to our world—as we have seen, in their own world they spend their time feasting.

In the old shamanic world view, the spirits of the ancestors were always hungry, and in Pagan Europe people satisfied that hunger by setting out food "for the faeries" or "for the elves" on particular nights. The elves or faeries were originally the vast community of the dead, the ancestors whose collective wisdom shapes the very archetypes that guide our souls, and when European peasants set out plates of food "for the elves," they were, in fact, feeding their ancestors.[12]

In that sense, the Queen of the Elves is but another face of the Old Life-and-Death Mother, she whom we have feared to meet. But as the Queen of Faery, she wears a mask of beauty rather than the twisted death mask of Badbh. To visit her may bring ecstasy as well as despair. We may remember that the Indian saint Ramakrishna meditated for years upon the bloodthirsty image of Kali before that goddess transformed herself, before his eyes, into a figure of great beauty.

We may also wish to remember just who it was, earlier in these pages, that emerged, like the Queen of the Elves, from a barrow mound, riding a spirit horse through the land....

This faery rider is, of course, Rhiannon herself, whom we have for the moment left back in the barrow mound, frozen to the Well of Memory. All women emerge from the realm of the Life-and-Death Mother. They all return to that realm at intervals. Not only do they meet the woman they most feared to meet, they actually become her.

This may be a transcendent experience indeed. No woman can aspire to the wisdom of the Sorceress or Crone until she has experienced that transformation.

This, then, is the beauty and the wisdom of the Shadow. Just as Perceval sought to slay the Red Knight—but learned, in the fullness of time, that he *was* the Red Knight—so we must learn to love and to embrace the Shadow, the hag aspect of the Life-and-Death Mother. It is precisely those aspects of ourselves that we hate the most that carry the seeds of our redemption.

Does that sound impossible? Can it be true that you, who have called yourself independent and yet generous, who have refused to recognize the greedy, whining little slut within, may be dependent on that darker, inferior self for your own growth and enlightenment?

Yes. It's true. Arianrhod may have fled from the court of Math in a rage, but her rage was the godchild of her desire for independence. She may have refused to help her child, but her fierce aloofness provided him with a more powerful initiation into manhood than he could ever have obtained with a simple blessing. She may have raged herself into oblivion at last, but even in her ending she embodied the spirit of divine rebellion and freedom.

What about the clinging creature that may lie beneath your independent exterior? Is she pointing toward your need for human contact, toward a compassion that your independent self is incapable of achieving alone? Could the greedy tightwad within perhaps become your greatest teacher in the art of self-control?

Yes, the Shadow points the way to redemption. No matter how she manifests herself for you personally, there will be, in most cases, a wild, fierce shadow indeed, with something of Arianrhod's sublime, free-spirited rebelliousness—for this is the reverse of the collective image of women as meek and mindless. Having experienced the touch of the elvish queen for herself, and having brought back treasures from the faery realms, a woman may well find herself somewhat at odds with the world around her. She may even wonder if she is mad, for the boundary between mental dysfunction and shamanic ecstasy is a thin one indeed. The mystic and the madwoman both have one foot in the land of the elves.

Due to the frequency with which she journeys in the Otherworld, the spiritual experience of the shamaness is beyond the ken of most individuals. Her mental and emotional development is altered—a different perspective exists regarding life's rites of passage. Thus women are likely to return from their spirit wanderings in a state of mind akin to craziness.

Take Cinderella, for instance, whose name, "Ella of the Cinders," is itself reminiscent of the ashes of the Underworld. Though we are all familiar with her "fairy godmother," there are earlier versions of her story in which she receives her good advice and her gifts from the bones of an animal which she has gathered together and over which she has sung magic songs. Whether by calling upon an animal totem or a "faery" ancestor, this worshipper of the Old Death Mother of Ashes is clearly receiving shamanic knowledge.[13] Thus she makes a shamanic journey to an Otherworldly Castle (one wonders if it was a revolving one) where she meets "the prince"—who, in some ancient version of the story, was surely the Prince of the Elves, the Lord of the Otherworld. But she returns to this world lacking one shoe.

One shoe off and one shoe on—Cinderella is, to use a scholarly term for it, asymmetrical. She is not quite merged with the dictates of reality. Or, to put it in a more colloquial way, she is quite literally "out of step."

So are all women who truly undertake the journey. Is this a reason for sadness, or for celebration?

Just as a shamaness is able to look beyond ordinary reality to touch upon the Otherworld, so the person manifesting a psychosis, or any unnatural detachment from reality, is likewise able to experience this other level of being. However, the psychotic's perceptions are chaotic and irrational, a parody of the truly mystical accomplishment of the shamaness. The shamaness may experience feelings of wholeness, cosmic oneness, and a sense of unity with all life that transcends time and space; by the same token, time and space also cease to have meaning for the mentally unbalanced person. The difference, however, is critical: the shamaness enters the Otherworld deliberately and returns to everyday life cognizant of the world at large, whereas the psychotic cannot separate daily, mundane life from the dream, and is forced to contend with the Otherworld while simultaneously trying to function in everyday reality.[14]

The human psyche is, at its most fundamental level, united with the whole universe and all of creation. When we are acting in a dysfunctional manner, however, our concept of universal wholeness—which, for women, may be imaged symbolically as a deep connection with the great barrow mound of the collective mind—is divided into disconnected fragments of thought and emotion. Therefore, in many ways we are more "normal" when we are acting upon strange, unwarranted impulses, for in so doing we are no longer repressed, split, or in denial, as we are when attempting to behave in a mode acceptable to any so-called "moral majority." Thus it may be said that the mentally unbalanced person is actually more closely in touch with her true feelings than she who is considered to be sane! By the same token, the shamanic personality is often somewhat removed from the ordinary social structure of the tribe; the shamaness or shaman displays different behavior from that which is deemed normal or common among the people.

In other words, Cinderella may be smeared with Underworld ashes and dancing with only one shoe, but she's dancing with the King of the Land of Youth.

While most tribal cultures view both the shamaness and the madwoman as someone who is sacred, blessed, and worthy of an honored place in the community, our own culture prefers to denigrate all those who are so touched by the Otherworld to the level of the mentally deranged.

People start to break when they lack a sense of belonging and cannot find their niche in life. The mind sometimes follows suit by over-reacting to that which it cannot assimilate. An individual's failure to adapt to the conditions in which she or he lives may occur for one of two reasons: the individual may be abnormal, or the environment may be abnormal.

The strong contemporary interest in shamanic techniques (including both Pagan European and Native American practices) owes a great deal to an abnormal environment—an environment that demands adherence to rigid puritanical standards in the context of an emotionally congested, sexually repressed culture. For those upon whom the doors to the Otherworld have slammed shut, the breezes that blow out carry only fear—most often expressed as a fear of the women and men who can slip into the Otherworld at will. It was a deep-seated fear of such Otherworldy empowerment that brought Europe to its knees during the Burning Times—in all probability, Isobel Gowdie died at the stake because of her elvish rambles. The same fear controls the majority of Americans today. Few realize that what was lost during the witch trials, along with the men, women, children, and animals that were put to death en masse, was the collective shamanic soul of the European people.[15] Our subsequent attempt to annihilate the American Indian has all but destroyed the chance for those of European ancestry to merge their consciousness with the collective mind of indigenous America. We may have conquered the land, but we cannot enter the doors to the Otherworldly kingdoms that lie hidden beneath our new, adopted earth.

Now those of us who hearken to the call of our ancestors are reminded of the old ways; we drink the waters of life from the well of rebirth in order to see our reflection more clearly, and remember. Still, we may feel the need to ask: Are we crazy if we walk against the flow of society?

No, for we are acting in the interest of self-preservation at a very instinctual level (though we may seem crazy to those who act in concert with an abnormal environment). In fact, we are closer to the reality of the natural order of things—at one with Nature herself.

Yet, when it comes to the actual descent into the well, it will be necessary for most of us to deal with the despair before we can achieve a shamanic breakthrough. The following exercise is a safe and effective way to meet with your shadow self, the madwoman and potential Dark Goddess of your soul.

Exercise III: Descent to Madness

Try this exercise more than once. You may be surprised at the number of personalities dwelling inside you, and the new and improved forms your madness can take. The madowoman within you may be smarter or less intelligent than your conscious self, crazier or saner than you had anticipated. She may even be a he; don't be surprised if the critter in your cave is a madman rather than a madwoman. We shall have more to say about this in the following chapter. But for the sake of convenience, we shall refer to the madperson in this exercise primarily as "she."

This is a complete technique in itself, and need not be combined with Exercise I (Purification Ritual) or Exercise II (The Otherworld Journey) in order to be effective. But as with Exercise II, you will want to keep your magical journal on hand to record the results. You may also wish to tape-record the entire exercise ahead of time, since there may be too many details to be remembered easily. In that event, you will of course be following the sound of your own voice into the world below.

First, make certain that you can remain undisturbed for at least twenty minutes. Lie down or sit comfortably. Begin to breathe deeply, drawing the air in through your nose and down into your belly. Hold it there for a moment and then release it through your mouth with an audible sigh. The sigh can be soft or loud, whichever feels more appropriate to you. Let go of all the tensions that have built up inside you. Feel the muscles of your body relax, especially those connected with your neck, shoulders, and eyes. Let your jaw go slack. Continue breathing in this way, releasing tension through your mouth with a sigh, until you feel completely relaxed. Now, continue to breathe through your nose only. Let your breath come regularly and naturally.

When you are ready to proceed, visualize yourself standing in a beautiful, peaceful open space, such as a flowery meadow or an endless sandy beach on the edge of the sea. How do you look? What are you wearing? Note the climate and season of this place; is it spring, summer, fall, or winter? Look around you. What do you see? As you gaze about this landscape, notice that there is a forest—at the edge of the meadow, just beyond the beach, or somewhere nearby. Begin to walk toward the trees. As you draw near, you see a narrow path leading into the thicket. Follow it. Soon you hear the sound of water. There is a small stream bubbling somewhere to your left. What else do you hear? Are birds singing, bees humming? What kind of animals live in this forest? Is there a muffled animal sound somewhere over to your right? If so, what kind of animal is it that follows alongside you as you move deeper into the woods—a hawk, a dog, a fox, a boar?

The path leads you onward until you come to a mound. You may imagine it as a natural hill of stone, or perhaps as a prehistoric barrow, like the one from which Rhiannon emerged, in which case it will be simply a mound of earth covered with grass and rocks. Observe it for a moment, until you spy a cleft in the natural rock or a doorway of stone in the barrow mound. This cave or doorway is your entry into the Otherworld, and you are about to go inside.

Enter the cave or barrow. Is it dark or light inside? As you go farther into the depths, you will come to a spiral stairway that circles down, far into the bowels of the earth. Take a deep breath, for you are about to descend the stairs.

Begin to descend, slowly and deliberately. Keep going, even though the stairway seemingly spirals down into an inky, black nothingness. Note the climate change as you descend the stair. Does the air grow colder or warmer? Is it clear and dry, or does it become musty and damp? What are you feeling? Are you nervous or bold? Finally, you reach level ground.

As your eyes adjust to the light, you realize that you are in a large corridor with two doors, one to your right and the other to your left. The door to your left is open. Walk over to it and peek inside. It is a room, but what kind of room? What epoch or era of time is reflected in the furnishings there? Is it bright, warm, and friendly, or dark, foreboding, and scary? Are the walls papered, painted, comprised of wood or stone? Are they adorned with paintings? If so, what kind? Are the floors carpeted, bare, covered with animal skins? Is there a hearth? If so, is there a fire burning in it? Are there furnishings in the room? Try to remember the details of this room, for a little later you will need to take another look inside and note if any changes have taken place.

Once you have seen what there is to see, turn around and face the other door. This door is shut, but you must now prepare to open it, to meet the madperson dwelling on the other side.

Walk over to the door and note how it is made. Now push it open and step inside, allowing it to close behind you.

What happens when you enter the room? Is your madperson shy or aggressive? Male or female? Does she or he jump out of the shadows in an attempt to frighten you, or languish forlornly in a corner of the room? Is she sitting up or lying down? How is she dressed? Is she neat or disheveled, rich or poor, elegant or crude?

How does this madwoman live? What does the room look like? Are there any animals about? If so, what kind are they and how do they respond to your madwoman, and to you?

If you have not already been approached by your madwoman, you must make the first move. Begin the dialogue by introducing yourself. Then ask for her name. Ask her how she arrived at this place and what she does there. Ask how she has come to be associated with you. Ask for her philosophy of life. Inquire as to her ideas concerning your life and how she thinks you should live it.

Now you must make a decision as to whether or not you want the madwoman to return from the Otherworld with you. If you feel that her particular form of madness (or wisdom) is not something that you would like to incorporate into your conscious, waking life, then politely take your leave of her when the time comes. But if you appreciate some of the qualities she embodies, and if you do want her help in the upper world, you must ask her to accompany you. If she is willing to make the journey, allow time for her to gather her things and say goodbye to her space below. Keep in mind that you are bringing a heretofore hidden aspect of your consciousness from darkness to light.

After you leave the madwoman's room and before you begin to ascend the stairs, take another look inside the door across the hall. Has anything changed in the room you saw when you first came down the stairs?

Remember the changes, if any, and begin the climb back to the world above. Note how you feel as you climb.

When you reach the top of the stairs, leave the cave or barrow mound the same way you entered. Climb down the slope and get back on the path that leads to the clearing. The stream should be on your right side now, and your madwoman should be with you, if this is what was agreed upon. Perhaps your power animal, if one followed you on your way into the forest, is still with you also.

Before you leave the forest, however, you must stop and make a deal with your madwoman. Find a good resting place somewhere along the bank of the stream. Tell your madwoman what you expect of her and see to it that she agrees to abide by your rules. She is in your world now and needs to behave herself. But also agree to be receptive to her ideas, thoughts, and emotions. She has a lot to teach you about yourself—and you have a lot to learn. When this agreement has been completed in a way that feels comfortable and safe to you, continue to move out of the woods and into the clearing where your adventure began. Feel the sensations of your body and focus once again on your breathing.

Slowly come back to full awareness and record your experience in your magical journal, remembering to note all the details.

Endnotes

1. Jeffrey Gantz, translator, *Early Irish Myths and Sagas* (Harmondsworth: Penguin, 1981).

2. C. G. Jung, "Aion: Phenomenology of the Self," in *The Portable Jung,* edited by Joseph Campbell (Harmondsworth: Penguin, 1980), 139-162.

3. Marguerite Elsbeth, unpublished poem.

4. Again, Celtic mythology is of special relevance here, for the "gifted but crazy artist" is a common Anglo-Saxon perception of the Celtic personality.

5. Samuel Taylor Coleridge, "Kubla Khan," in W. H. Auden and Norman Holmes Pearson, editors, *Romantic Poets* (New York: Viking Press, 1969), 152.

6. Sylvia Brinton Perera, *Descent to the Goddess: A Way of Initiation for Women* (Toronto: Inner City Books, 1981).

7. Kenneth Johnson, *North Star Road,* 61-88.

8. Mircea Eliade, *Shamanism: Archaic Techniques of Ecstasy* (Princeton: Princeton-Bollingen, 1972).

9. "Erik the Red's Saga," in *The Vinland Sagas: The Norse Discovery of America,* translated by Magnus Magnusson and Herman Palssen (Baltimore: Penguin, 1965), 81-83.

10. Johnson, *North Star Road.*

11. Ibid., 74-76.

12. Ibid., *passim.*

13. Ibid., 71-72.

14. Michael Talbot, *The Holographic Universe* (New York: HarperCollins, 1992), 63-65.

15. Johnson, *North Star Road.*

CHAPTER EIGHT

Dancing with the
Otherworld King

The dance is a circle in the time-space continuum of life—ever-flow-ing, eternal energy, a process of becoming, the passage of universal time, the physical incarnation of the Great Round of Nature itself.

An earlier generation of women feared Nature's wildness, and sought to tame the forests into farms even as they sought to tame their own inner wildness into cultivated domesticity. Now, in a world of cold steel and sharp glass, we long for Nature once again. We long for the Wild Woman within, the rebel shamaness who stands at odds to our collective image of womanhood.

This is one of the factors that makes Celtic myth, in particular, so relevant to contemporary women. Celtic mythology is exceptionally rich in the archetype of the Wild Woman. Arising from the great barrow mound where she sleeps, the vital creative force of the earth itself, she bursts into the daylight world, still rich and vivid with the ferocity of Nature. She may wield the knife, show her teeth, and dance in joy as she slaughters us; like the Old Hag of Beare, she may moan like the wind over the rocky seashore because she has grown old and loathly. Yet she will bloom again, young and lovely and sensual like the spring... but forever wild.

She is love and war, sex and death, a flowering meadow and a barren headland, a summer's day and a raging storm all rolled into one. No wonder she frightens us. No wonder most men don't know what to do with her.

This fearsome "she" has many faces. We have met her in the guise of Blodeuwedd, the "woman made of flowers" who, as a result of denying her shadow self, tried to murder her husband Llew and thus became the Terrible Lover. The pregnant and seemingly passive Macha ran like a horse and, as she lay dying on the ground, cursed the heroes of the Red Branch with the pangs of childbirth. Queen Maeve was a goddess sufficiently powerful to survive until nearly recent times, for though we met her in an earlier chapter as a wild queen, she was remembered in Shakespeare's time (and until the present day by isolated countryfolk in the Western Irish county of Sligo) as Mab, the Queen of Faery.[1] The witch Cerridwen kept the cauldron of inspiration, between bouts of shapeshifting and running about as an old wild hag. And let us not forget the Morrigan, the raven goddess who brings death and destruction to all.

The Morrigan is familiar to most of us as Morgan le Fay, the sorceress who conveyed the wounded King Arthur to the Otherworldly Isle of Avalon, and indeed the Old Dark Goddess appears throughout the courtly medieval legends of Arthur and his knights. There is the voracious, power-mad Queen Morgause; there is Iseult, a temperamental sorceress as well as a temperamental lover. Lady Elaine, the "lily maid" of Astolat, went mad when spurned by Lancelot.

The women who inhabit Celtic mythology are forces of Nature. They all dance on the edge of madness, and many of them are the literary descendants of goddesses who, like Hindu Kali, come raging out of the Revolving Castle with a howl and a shriek and a mouthful of bloody fangs. Even Rhiannon, a relatively sweet creature, was taken by the earth and sky and sent back to the depths from whence she came.

Recognizing our kinship with the wild women of ancient Celtic lore, we may take heart that a harrowing journey to the depths of the Otherworld will bring us, in time, to a light that shines like a fierce and sudden rainbow over a wild thicket of forest. We may console ourselves with the notion that all women, at one time or another, must make the journey.

*This is how a
woman—
first maiden,
then mother—
becomes a crone.
She faces the oldest
crone of all,
and learns from her.*

But the question remains: with so many dark places and pitfalls in the depths of the well, how shall we find our way back to the light?

This is how Rhiannon returned from the Otherworld[2]....

Cigfa was anxious now that Pryderi and Rhiannon were gone and she and Manawydan would be alone in the court. She need not have worried about her virtue, however, because Manawydan, upon seeing her distress, vowed to be her true and loyal friend. Together the two of them traveled about while Manawydan earned their keep as a shoemaker.

Bringing with him a burden of wheat, Manawydan eventually led them back to Dyfed. He set up a dwelling place in Arberth, where he and Pryderi had once hunted. There he hunted again, and fished and tilled the soil. Soon he sowed three crofts of wheat, and the wheat that grew was the finest in the land.

Harvest time came and Manawydan set out into the grey dawn to check his fields. He arrived at the first of the three crofts and decided to reap it on the morrow, for the wheat was golden ripe. But alas, when he returned the next day, the ears had been broken off and carried away, leaving only the naked stalks!

This left him wondering, so he went to see the second of his crofts. Here the wheat was ripe also and again he decided to reap on the following day. Come sunrise, Manawydan returned to the croft only to find naked stalks where ripened wheat had been. Convinced that someone was completing his ruin, he took up watch that night in the third croft.

All was quiet until midnight, when there arose a great commotion. Manawydan looked up to see the mightiest host of mice in the world, so many he could not count them all. He watched as the mice fell upon the croft, breaking off the ears, making off with them and leaving only bare stalks behind.

Anger washed over him and he rushed in amidst the mice, but he could not train his eye on one long enough to catch it. Finally he spied a mouse that was heavier and therefore slower than the others. He went after it, caught it, put it in his glove, and carried it to the court.

"I have caught a thief," Manawydan said to Cigfa upon his return.

"What kind of thief fits into a glove?" Cigfa asked.

Manawydan then explained to Cigfa all that had happened. His plan was to hang the mouse on the very next day. Though Cigfa begged him not to do it, Manawydan went on with his plan.

Manawydan made for the mound of Gorsedd Arberth with the mouse and planted two forks on the highest point of the mound. As he prepared the little gallows, he saw a clerk dressed in threadbare clothing approach. This was the first person Manawydan had seen in Dyfed since it had been laid to waste. The man conversed with Manawydan, imploring him to let the mouse go, but Manawydan was intent on hanging the thief and the man gave up and went on his way.

Again Manawydan resumed his work on the gallows, fixing the crossbeam across the forks, when he saw a priest ride up on a horse. The priest tried to convince Manawydan that it was beneath his dignity and rank to hang a mouse, but Manawydan would hear none of it and soon the priest went away.

He was fastening the noose around the neck of the mouse and drawing it up when he saw a bishop and his retinue coming up the mound. This time Manawydan kept to his work. Like the clerk and the priest, the bishop asked Manawydan to let the mouse go. Manawydan refused. The bishop then tried to offer Manawydan money in exchange for the creature. More and more money was offered, and the baggage and horses and retinue also, but Manawydan would have none of it.

"Name your price," said the bishop.

"That Rhiannon and Pryderi be set free, that the enchantment be removed from the seven cantrevs of Dyfed, and that I am told the identity of this mouse."

"I am Llwyd, son of Cil Coed," said the bishop, "I cast the enchantment over Dyfed because Gwawl, son of Clud, is my friend, and to avenge him I enchanted Pryderi, son of Pwyll, Head of Annwn, for the time Pwyll played at Badger-in-the-Bag with Gwawl, and for his taking of Rhiannon from the court of Heveydd the Old. The mouse is my wife and she is with child. I will give you Rhiannon and Pryderi, and take the enchantment off Dyfed. Let her go!"

"I will not let her go until you also promise never to harm me, Rhiannon, or Pryderi because of this. Also, I must see them standing here with me."

Then Manawydan saw Rhiannon and Pryderi approach. He greeted them and they all sat down; he looked about and saw that once again the people, dwellings, and herds of Dyfed were restored.

When Manawydan asked Llwyd what had befallen Rhiannon and Pryderi during their time in the Otherworld, he was told that Pryderi had carried the gate-hammers of the court about his neck while Rhiannon wore the collars of asses after the beasts had been gathering hay.

One would like to assume that they all lived happily ever after....

Scholars have called the tale of Rhiannon's return one of the most confused and mystifying passages in medieval Welsh literature. If it points out the road back from the Otherworld, then that road must be a dark and winding one indeed. Let us take a look at some of the themes and archetypes that lie along the path.

At least part of the symbolism of the story is already familiar to us. For example, the fact that Rhiannon wears the halters of beasts of burden may remind us of her time in the horse block. We may remember that the Old Life-and-Death Mother makes us work hard and keep quiet, like the girl in the Mother Hulda story, so it is not surprising that Rhiannon, during her latest visit to the Ancient Mother's realm, has once again labored in silence. This is as it should be.

We may wonder at the presence of a fellow named Llwyd in a realm which we have come to associate exclusively with the Dark Goddess. Some of us may be slightly (or greatly) annoyed that Rhiannon seems to need a man—her husband Manawydan—to help her return from the Otherworld in one piece. Is this just another example of men muscling their loutish way into a mystery that ought, by rights, to be reserved for women?

Perhaps not. For all the men in this story are, in fact, dwellers in the great barrow mound—figures in Rhiannon's unconscious and archetypal actors in her personal myth.

Rhiannon, we may remember, journeyed to the Underworld in search of her son, Pryderi. For his sake she jumped down the magic Well of Memory and Fate that leads to the Old Birth-and-Death Mother's realm. But her search for Pryderi is, in fact, nothing less than a search for her own Divine Self.

In Chapter 4, we learned that the Divine Child is often a metaphor for the higher, more enlightened consciousness which lies within all of us and which is called the Self. Yet, for most of us, the Self exists only in a state of latent potentiality—throughout most of our lives, it remains asleep within us and must be properly awakened in order to become the guiding factor in our lives. This awakening of the Self is like a birth—in mythic terms, the birth of the Divine Child. The Divine Child is not the same as the sniveling, tantrum-prone darling of pop psychology, your Inner Child. The birth of the Self is like a sunrise in the darkness of the unawakened soul; thus, psychologically speaking, it is no accident that the Divine Child of the Christian myth is born at the winter solstice, the precise moment when the sun's power is reborn in the darkness of winter. Pryderi, then, is more than just the physical child to whom Rhiannon gave birth; he is the Divine Child of her higher Self, and she journeyed back into the Revolving Castle in order to awaken that Self.

Though the story in the *Mabinogion* passes in silence over Rhiannon's time in the Underworld—save to note that she wore an asses' collar—we may be certain that she encountered the Old Bone Mother there in the depths. None of us may experience the birth of the Self unless we have fearlessly and honestly faced the Shadow and, ultimately, embraced her as part of ourselves. The Bone Mother is always waiting for us, holding up the mirror of our own darker nature and revealing to us a raging hag smeared with blood and sporting fangs. Until we have looked her in the face, seen ourselves in (and through) her eyes, and acknowledged her as part of our totality, we may not proceed to the deeper waters of Memory's Well. The Bone Mother forces us to work in silence, a deep spiritual silence that is nothing less than a death and rebirth. It is no wonder, then, that the Dark Goddess, in all cultures, is she who initiates us by slaying our illusions.

Very well, then. Rhiannon has descended to the depths in search of her Self, and she has met the Life-and-Death Mother, seen and accepted the raging core of wild womanhood that lies at the center of Arianrhod's silver wheel. But the story passes over the Dark Goddess with nary a word, and presents us instead with a fellow named Llwyd, who is apparently a good buddy of Rhiannon's old nemesis Gwawl. In terms of the archetypes and mythic figures who inhabit the magic well of Rhiannon's soul, who is he?

Most Western mythologies postulate two rulers in the Otherworld, a king and a queen. Speaking from an historical point of view, feminist scholars have argued that the Goddess cultures of ancient Europe recognized only an Otherworld Queen; the fact that the goddess Hel ruled the Norse Underworld all alone, as did her folkloric successor Mother Hulda, would seem to bear this out, as does a Sumerian legend which chronicles how the god Nergal swept into the Underworld and forced the goddess Ereshkigal (Ishtar's slimy-haired initatrix) to share her throne with him.

The tale of Nergal and Ereshkigal, in fact, relates, in mythic language, an episode that probably took place all over ancient Europe and the Near East. The Indo-European warriors who invaded and conquered the Goddess-centered cultures at the beginning of the Bronze Age worshipped a Lord of the Underworld rather than a Lady. His original name may have been something like Yemos, which means "twin," for in those most ancient days he was regarded as the twin of Dyaus, the god of the shining sky. A twin, and yet different: one king ruled in the bright clarity of the sky, the other in the dark Underworld. Dyaus of the Shining Sky ruled over the daylight world of consciousness; Yemos the Twin ruled over the nightworld of dreams and visions, as well as over the fertility of the earth above him.[3] The Otherworld is a mirror image of our own; everything is the same, though in exact reverse. Night mirrors day, Shadow mirrors Self, and vice versa.

The patriarchal conquest of Europe did not occur overnight; it took many generations, and was accomplished by intermarriage and agreement as often as by war. Thus, as feminist historian Marija Gimbutas claimed,[4] the mythologies of Pagan Europe are composites, retaining elements of the Goddess cultures alongside purely Indo-European elements. The Indo-European Lord of the Underworld married the solitary Life-and-Death Mother of the Goddess cultures. So there are two rulers in the Otherworld.

Whatever one may think of all this from an historical point of view, the double rulership of the elvish realms contains a profound psychological truth, for we are all androgynous in consciousness, in the spirit. After a woman has gazed in the reverse mirror of the Otherworld and seen her own Shadow in the form of the Dark Goddess, she is ready to encounter the great "twin" who dwells in the deepest part of her soul—the Otherworld King, he who first presented himself as the Demon Lover.

The Demon Lover is a spell caster. As we have seen, he first appears in women's lives as a rather frightening fellow, but one who is curiously seductive. In early life, a woman's relationships with real men are usually colored by the allure of the Demon Lover, which is why such relationships so often go wrong—after all, there can be no permanent union between the elvish kingdom and our own. If a woman is practical and strong, however, like Janet in the folksong "Tam Lin," she may succeed in breaking the Demon Lover's spell long enough to see a man as he really is. If she is wise as well as strong, she may even do so rather early in life. However, this is just the first step. In order to transform the Demon Lover into the inner partner of her own soul, a woman must wrestle with Tam Lin again and again, for it is unlikely that she will completely succeed in transforming the Demon Lover much before the middle years of her life.

Why not? Because the Demon Lover often clothes himself in the same vestments as his queen, the Old Bone Mother, and until a woman has faced her own Shadow she simply does not possess the psychological equipment necessary to transform the Demon Lover.

In Rhiannon's case, we know that she has had more than a few issues with the Demon Lover. Years ago, she had her champion cudgel old Gwawl and stick him in a bag. Now Gwawl has taken his revenge through his friend Llwyd, the Underworld King. We can see that Rhiannon is facing the Demon Lover once again, and that Llwyd, like Pryderi, actually represents a portion of her own soul.

Important as the Demon Lover is, however, a woman need not engage him in an actual wrestling match, as Janet did with Tam Lin, for this will succeed only in removing his spell from her own relationships with men. She is still a long way from the end of the game.

What, then, is the end of the game?

In the previous chapter, we explored the shamanic roots of the Cinderella fairytale—a universal story that is found not only in Celtic countries but very, very far beyond. Cinderella, the girl with ashes on her face, has been forced to do hard labor in the Bone Mother's dark school. Helped by the reconstituted bones of an animal she has nurtured and cherished, she journeys to the hall of the prince, where she joins with him in a dance. We know that she is actually in the Otherworld, for she comes home with only one shoe—she has been touched by the curious reverse mirror of the Otherworld and her own relationship with worldly reality is now slightly out of sync or asymmetrical. Cinderella, then, has been dancing with the Otherworld King.

This is the goal: a woman's relationship with the animus, the male half of her own soul, should be like a dance. When Beauty danced with the Beast in his magic castle in the forest, she too was dancing with the Otherworld King.

This image is a universal one, and survives even in present-day pop culture. In Tim Burton's cult film *Edward Scissorhands,* a young girl named Kim, played by Winona Ryder, enters a sad and stormy relationship with Edward, the patchwork, "unfinished" creation of a mad scientist. Until now, Edward has lived alone in a dark castle above a mythic American town. He descends from his Otherworld lair but encounters nothing but trouble—as we know, the rules are reversed on the other side of the mirror. The town itself exists in an artificial world of light; it is always warm there, and the people have never seen snow. Neither do they recognize their own darker sides, and hence they alternately praise and reject the elvish boy with scissors for hands. When Edward longs to sculpt Kim's figure in ice, he wills the snow into being. Emerging from her house into a backyard that has now been rendered Otherworldly, Kim sees snow falling in the night and Edward carving madly in a shower of ice. In a scene that constitutes the most transcendent moment in the film, she dances enraptured in the snow. And though in time Edward must return to his Otherworld castle, Kim has been forever transformed by the experience; as an aged crone, she whispers ecstatically to her granddaughter: "Sometimes when it snows, you can still catch me dancing."

If the earth is a sphere, then the abyss below the earth is also its heavens; and the difference between them is no more than time, the time of the earth's turning.[5]

The dance, one of the most ancient forms of magic, was originally an act of creation wherein the dancer was metamorphosized into some other chosen form of existence, such as a goddess, an animal, or an elemental being. The dance is a circle in the time-space continuum of life—ever-flowing, eternal energy, a process of becoming, the passage of universal time, the physical incarnation of the Great Round of Nature itself. So we dance the spirit dance, turning with the earth's purpose, our eyes seeing all and nothing as we share our vision with the eyes of the soul.

Thus we may fully experience, express, and embody the Demon Lover through the music, rhythms, and actions of our own integral wholeness. Like a shamaness, we may now pass from the plane of ordinary reality into the Otherworld reality of both the individual and collective mind.

However, in order to do this successfully, we must bring ourselves to believe that such a passage has actually taken place by asking ourselves questions such as: If I were really Janet or Beauty or Kim, how would I react? What would I do? We must become one with the Demon Lover through the sincerity of our emotions and have faith that what we are doing is real. This is the magic created by the shamaness, shape-shifting and healing both inner and outer circumstances in herself, in others, and in the world at large. This, ultimately, is the magic we can create within ourselves when we reconnect with the Demon Lover, allow his spirit to lead us out of our own inner darkness, and continue to live his essential nature throughout the moments of our lives.

To embody the archetype of the Demon Lover through spirit dancing is to experience a blessing. It allows us to understand even our smallest physical, emotional, mental, and spiritual needs, and soothes our individual fears, personal losses, and private anxieties. Dancing the spirit of our male shadow—or of our inner Torch Bearer—brings us vision, inspiration, imagination, and a new sense of the ultimate muse which is the Self. Thus the spirit dancer transcends the ordinary world, while yet owning the operations, mechanisms, and motivations of material existence.

Dancing the dance allows us to become our own lover, because self and not-self motivates its movements. Imagine the heady fascination of that: to project back at ourselves all of the romantic captivation, moonstruck infatuation, and obsessive idealism we usually reserve for the object of our devotion. What could possibly be more effective in attracting the healthy sort of relationship most of us desire than to do so from such a self-aware, self-loving standpoint?

Because the animus first appears to us wearing the dark vestments of his Bone Mother bride—which is to say, as the Demon Lover, the fairytale Beast, or crippled Edward—we must first confront the Shadow and transform the Dark Goddess herself. Then the Demon Lover will likewise drop his fierce mask and reveal himself in beauty. Like Psyche in the Greek myth (discussed in Chapter 2), we will someday hold up a silent candle and see him as he really is—a god, the inner god in everywoman's soul.

It is only through quiet service to the Bone Mother herself that this may be accomplished. When Psyche gazed too soon upon the godlike face of Eros, he fled. In order to regain him, she was forced to perform a number of impossible tasks in the service of Aphrodite—tasks resembling those that, in a Slavic fairytale, were performed by the girl called Vassilisa the Wise in the service of Baba Yaga, the wild "cannibal witch" who is also the initiator of women. Cinderella too served her time in the Bone Mother's greasy kitchen, as did the girl who traveled down the well to Mother Hulda's realm.

When a woman has done all these things, performed all these tasks, and learned how to see the Dark Goddess in her robe of beauty, a marvelous transformation takes place. The Beast becomes a prince, and he carries in his hands a torch with which to guide you through the darkness. Psyche borrowed his torch when she gazed upon Eros in the darkness. Theseus carried a torch through the labyrinth of Crete, and slew the fearsome minotaur that haunted Ariadne's soul. Who carried a torch to lead Beauty through the dark, labyrinthine hallways of the enchanted castle? The Beast himself.

The torch he carries is the torch of a woman's *logos,* the other half of her soul. As long as the Beast remains a beast, a woman may be sure that she is still in the world of *eros*—her natural world and true home, to be sure, but still only half of the Self's totality, a yin without a yang. When the monster at last becomes a godly torch bearer—which is possible only after the Dark Goddess has slain all the "monsters" of our illusions—a woman is complete, for she has learned how to dance with the *logos.* Yin and yang are now altogether entwined in the wholeness of her being. Thus the Torch Bearer of our soul may lead us out of the labyrinth of the Revolving Castle, back into the world of light.

This, finally, is Manawydan's role in the tale of Rhiannon. He brings Rhiannon's spirit to light. As we have seen, the Children of Llyr are often associated with the old earth-and-sea deities of the Otherworld, and Manawydan is a son of Llyr. In Irish lore, he has a slightly different name, which is Manannan mac Lir—this Manannan was remembered in Ireland, even till the end of the seventeenth century, as the king of the "Land of Youth." Manawydan himself, then, is the Otherworld King. Acting as Rhiannon's torch-bearing *logos,* he charms her back out of the dark realms.

This is how a woman—first maiden, then mother—becomes a crone. She faces the oldest crone of all, and learns from her. What she learns is completeness, imaged in myth as a transcendent spirit dance with the torch-bearing animus of her soul.

Now she is truly ready for wisdom. Now she is ready to become a Sorceress.

Exercise IV: Dreamwork

By entering into a relationship with the Demon Lover, you can teach yourself how to dance with him. But how may such a relationship be established?

Our Pagan ancestors were much closer to the Otherworld than most of us are today. Their visions were made manifest in their ordinary lives, taking shape in the form of omens, dreams, and mystical experiences. In many ancient stories, a mortal might experience the visit of an Otherworldly mate or bride in the form of an intense and powerful vision—like Janet, who struggles with her elvish lover Tam Lin, or like the male figures of Celtic myth who, guided by an Otherworldly woman (who is none other than their own anima or spirit bride), journey to the Land of Youth.

For most of us today, the most effective way to receive messages from the Otherworld is through dreams. You may think of a dream as something that simply happens to you, something over which you have no control. To a certain extent this is true. However, some very talented individuals are able to achieve "lucid dreaming," and hence shape their own dreams with full knowledge of what they're doing. Most of us experience dreams as sudden (and sometimes intrusive) messages from our own unconscious minds. The dream speaks the language of the barrow mound.

Nevertheless, we may participate in our own dreams to a greater degree than most of us realize. We can even learn to become acquainted with the Demon Lover within us, and to assist in his transformation to the Torch Bearer of the Soul with whom we dance in the Otherworld.

First, you must learn to remember your dreams. Though some people do this quite naturally and without any effort, most of us have to struggle with it. The best way is as follows.

As you begin to fall asleep at night, repeat to yourself, over and over again, that you remember all your dreams. (Don't affirm that you *will* remember, because this puts things in the future tense; affirm that you *do* remember.) You may have to go through many unsuccessful nights before the affirmation begins to work, but after a while it will.

When it begins to work, be ready! Keep a notebook or tape recorder next to your bed. Record your dreams as soon as you wake up. If you wake up in the middle of the night, never assume that you will remember your dream in the morning, because you probably won't. Just turn on the light and write it down.

After a few weeks of writing down your dreams, you should be able to identify the Demon Lover. He may not look the same in every dream, but he will act the same. He may appear as a rock star, a social rebel, or simply a "mystery man." If you have some really difficult issues with men or if you are carrying a great deal of unrealized darkness within you (trying to get away from Old Boney again, eh?), he may appear as a psychopath, terrorist, or stalker. More rarely, he may appear as an animal, usually a horse.

At first, you may not want to remember your dream encounters with the Otherworld King. After all, who really wants to think about being stalked through dark city streets by a demented psychopath with a bloody knife? Don't be afraid. Keep remembering and writing things down.

The next step is the most difficult. You will need to meditate on those dreams in which the Demon Lover makes his spooky appearances. Then you need to ask yourself: What is he telling me about myself?

This is the most difficult step because it necessitates facing your own inner darkness. Remember, it's not him (or any other man) who is the source of your problems. He is a component of your own soul—the difficulties are yours. If all men seem like vicious animals to you, or if you regard the "evil male principle" as being responsible for the ills of the world, you will probably need to do a great deal of dreamwork in order to gain a clear vision of the Torch Bearer within.

The Demon Lover guards the gates to the Bone Mother's kingdom. He may speak his dark, unwelcome wisdom very directly—the stalker or terrorist may suddenly lay down his machine gun and speak words of wisdom in a dream—or you may have to learn, through consistent meditation, what his strange actions and mysterious utterances really mean. In any event, the answer will probably send you back to Mother Hulda's cottage for another session of spiritual housecleaning.

In time, however, you will notice some changes beginning to occur in your dream journal. As you progress with your silent work of the soul, the Demon Lover will start to look less like Freddy Kruger and more like Sir Lancelot. Then you will know that you are making progress.

Then you will be ready for the dance.

Exercise V: Spirit Dancing

The Otherworld King is not separate from you; rather, he is part of you. To dance with him is to dance with yourself. Such a dance can only occur when you are dancing the deepest aspects of your own soul.

To dance your own deep soul is to spirit dance. But since our true Spirit Self has ostensibly gone into hiding, we may first need to ask ourselves a vital question: Who am I?

The dreamwork described above will bring about this question quite naturally—in fact, inevitably. That doesn't make it any easier to find an answer.

When our Spirit Self isn't dancing because our false self is running the show, it is difficult to know who we are, possibly as hard as knowing what it is we really want out of life. (Of course, if we knew who we were in the first place, we'd know what we wanted, wouldn't we?)

So how do we go about recovering our own inner Spirit Dancer, our wild and wondrous Self—and then, beyond that, recapturing the best dancing partner we'll ever know, the Demon Lover, our torch-bearing Spirit Self?

We can start by learning how we pretend to be who we are not, and then not pretending anymore. Complete the following sentences about your imposter self:

> 1. I make-believe I am ....
>
> 2. My friends and acquaintances don't realize that I ....
>
> 3. I seem to be ..., but that's not what I'm feeling inside.
>
> 4. The real me is hidden by ....

Now complete the following sentences with answers about your real self:

> 1. I feel most like myself when ....
>
> 2. I believe most strongly in ....
>
> 3. My goal in life is ....
>
> 4. The memory I hold most dear is ....

Elaborate on these ideas. Write down any additional thoughts that come to mind. Then consciously, fearlessly remove the frozen mask covering the real self and begin to re-ensoul the image that is really you.

Remember, there is no such thing as death when the inner vision of the Self is healed, for the spirit is eternal and the circle dance wheels round and round forever, spiraling outward beyond Caer Arianrhod's Revolving Castle of the North Wind.

Perform the written exercise above a few times, in conjunction with your dreamwork. Then you will be ready to dance your inner Self. As before, you will need a rattle; a drum and a drumming partner or a drumming tape; a quiet, private, roomy space free from interruptions and preferably outdoors (although this is not necessary).

Lie down on the earth, or indoors in a comfortable spot. Have your rattle and drum tape close at hand. Relax. Open your senses to the elements around and under you—fiery sun, breeze-kissed sky, water running underground, the earth buoying you up while holding you down.

Close your eyes. Take a deep breath and exhale loudly, releasing the tension held in your body to the earth beneath you. Do this three more times. Now become increasingly more aware of the earth's gravity pulling your body down like a magnet while simultaneously filling you with energy from its molten core.

When you feel that your body is filled to overflowing with vital earth force, sit or stand up. Using all your powers of imagination, step out of your body and face yourself. (This need not be a genuine "out-of-body" or astral experience, which can be dangerous for the inexperienced. You may simply keep your eyes closed and imagine yourself looking back at your body.)

Reaching forward with spirit hands, begin to shape and mold your body into the spirit you feel you truly are. You may become whatever creature or thing best exemplifies your image of yourself, whether this happens to be a Celtic goddess such as Rhiannon or Arianrhod, an animal such as the eagle, wolf, deer, or rabbit, or even a tree such as oak, hazel, or rowan. Remember to include all the qualities of the spirit you are taking on—physical, emotional, mental, and spiritual.

When you are finished transforming yourself in imagination, mentally have your spirit self step back into your new spirit body. Now it is time to spirit dance. Take up your rattle and shake it in tune to the rhythm held in your spirit body. (If you are using a drumming tape, turn it on and begin to move slowly to the rhythm of the drum.) Let your spirit body be your guide. At this time, your drumming partner should begin drumming, following the pace set by the rhythm and speed at which you shake your rattle. She or he should continue to follow your pace throughout the balance of the dance.

The movements of the dance are dependent on how the "spirit" moves you. Give yourself up to it, let your spirit soar, lope, rush, charge, jump, or buck. Grunt, snort, howl, or sing, if your spirit body wishes to express itself in voice.

Do not attempt to judge the time of the dance; it will be different for everyone. Just dance until your spirit body is finished dancing.

When you are done, lie back down on the earth and relax. Feel your spirit body gently release into the earth as you become increasingly aware of your physical body. Thank the earth and your spirit body for dancing you.

If you continue to seek your Self and to spirit dance her in all her glory, as well as seeking your inner Torch Bearer through dreamwork, you will discover that, in time, something unusual will begin to happen—you will no longer be alone in your spirit dancing. Someone will be dancing with you, keeping step with you, perhaps even taking the role of the active partner, leading you on.

You know who he is.

Endnotes

1. Graves, *The White Goddess,* 105.

2. Gantz, *Mabinogion,* 90-96.

3. J. P. Mallory, *In Search of the Indo-Europeans* (London and New York: Thames and Hudson, 1994), 128-142.

4. See especially *The Civilization of the Goddess: The World of Old Europe* (San Francisco, Harper Collins, 1991), 352-401.

5. Maya Deren, *Divine Horsemen: The Voodoo Gods of Haiti* (New York, Chelsea House Publishers, 1970), 260.

CHAPTER NINE

The Queen of Avalon

Whenever a woman has danced with the Otherworld King in the Revolving Castle of her soul and then retuned to the world of light, she has attained to something of the wisdom of the Crone. It matters not whether she herself is young or old, for she has undergone a passage, a transformation, and she can never be quite the same—she will never be innocent or foolish again.

THE BONE MOTHER, frightening though she may seem, places herself at our disposal whenever we take the spiritual path; if we choose to misuse or ignore her teachings, there is no turning back. We are told, in no uncertain terms, to use it or lose it. Therefore, whenever we are forced headlong into the Underworld, we face, again and again, that great and heroic choice: We can allow the Life-and-Death Goddess to purify our souls or we can remain spiritually, creatively, and emotionally bankrupt as a result of our inability to change.

Whenever a woman has danced with the Otherworld King in the Revolving Castle of her soul and then retuned to the world of light, she has attained to something of the wisdom of the Crone. It matters not whether she herself is young or old, for she has undergone a passage, a transformation, and she can never be quite the same—she will never be innocent or foolish again. Now the Bone Mother stands forever at her side and whispers wisdom into her ear. Such a woman has learned to live asymmetrically, side by side with the Otherworldly.

Every woman, whether or not she has walked the wilder chambers of the Silver Wheel, experiences a time when she is fertile, ripe, and naturally in season. A woman who has been transformed in the Otherworld consciously chooses her season, her power time. To use the ancient Pagan festivals as psychological metaphors, a woman may choose the path of Beltane, the May Day of the soul, if she desires to be enchanted by sunlit meadows, gentle breezes, and the heady aroma of the flower-strewn earth. Or, should she wish to live her life in misty shadows and the veiled darkness of mystery, truth, and wisdom (a choice far more adventurous than the decision to dwell above-ground under the glowing auspices of the daystar), she may orient her Wild Woman spirit toward the waning October dream of Samhain. Either way, she must continually meet up with death, whether as fearsome shadow or as treasured friend—so in a sense the choice is already made for her.

Those who choose the daylight and the flowers may prefer to be taken unaware—though conscious of the Bone Mother's presence, they turn their faces away from her, toward the light of the sun. Rhiannon, for example, was not a Wild Woman at heart. Even though she emerged from a cleft in the great barrow mound of Gorsedd Arberth, she came with the intention of marrying Pwyll—of entering into relationship. Thus she must have realized that by choosing this common but difficult path she would need to give up a part of her Otherworldly self. Maybe she didn't realize that it would have to be that way. Perhaps she just eventually forgot about the faery side of her nature, as so many of us do when we take on the responsibilities and obligations of marriage and all the domestic duties associated with that institution. But unless a woman has a strong, well-developed ego, her delicate psyche—and hence her innate Otherworldliness—may very well be compromised or even obliterated as a result.

No woman is born devoid of a Wild Woman self. Our visit to Arianrhod's Castle, and to the madwoman's bony dwelling place at the center of things, has taught us that the Wild Woman is the very root, heart, and soul of a woman's being. It is from this free and wild spirit that a woman derives sustenance, and it is to the weedy, unruly, overgrown, uncultivated,

No woman is born devoid of a Wild Woman self. Our visit to Arianrhod's Castle, and to the madwoman's bony dwelling place at the center of things, has taught us that the Wild Woman is the very root, heart, and soul of a woman's being.

primitive nature sleeping inside herself that a woman must someday return, ready or not, just as Rhiannon was forced to return to the misty barrows despite her choice to live out her days in the bright and shining upper world.

A woman who chooses to embrace relationship and all its requisite attributes—including attraction, affection, love, beauty, harmony, desirability, profundity, and domesticity—must naturally make the Wild Woman a part of her shadow self. "As above, so below"—to surround ourselves with daylight is to place the wild darkness, its polar opposite, squarely in one's darkest mirror, a harsh if necessary reflection. Such a woman is therefore bound to be reintroduced, against her will but again and again, to that old solitary, the Bone Mother, in order to undergo painful reconstruction, purgation, purification, and spiritual upliftment.

Basically, every woman has a choice: "Transform or die," Old Bony tells us. "Arise to the heights of womanly greatness or join the dregs of female humanity. Resist my influence and stagnate forevermore."

What of those who glory in the darkness and willingly dwell with the Dark Goddess who, with her raucous croak and feathery-cloaked black raven-wing arms aching to enfold our senses in eternal night, waits at the crossroads?

We have seen how the Dark Mother transforms us in the netherworld, how she teaches us through suffering, so that we may understand the wisdom of death, of transformation. Is there something else in her teaching, beyond the ultimate initiatory experience of separating the spiritual essence from the physical body? How does the Wild Woman greet her when she comes plucking at the meat on our bones? Does the Ancient One offer only death?

Perhaps it seems preposterous that we should look for something more than the experience of physical release. After all, how many of us really understand or know firsthand the actual sensation of completely leaving this flesh behind—meditations, journeys, and life-after-life notwithstanding?

Nevertheless, we do seek something more, and as long as we live, we seek. Though we have come to know the Bone Mother in various forms, we have only touched briefly on the most formidable of Celtic mythology's dark goddesses, the spirit called the Morrigan. Let us now make her acquaintance at more length, and see what she has to teach us.

The Morrigan is an older deity than the light-bearing Children of Danu and Don. She is the goddess of the land, and one Samhain when the gods still walked in Ireland, she straddled a river so that the prodigious and priapic god called the Dagda could mate with her and produce yet another great Irish river, the Boyne. Yet she is also the horrific spirit who haunts the battlefields in the guise of a raven. When warriors see a woman washing their bloody clothes at a river, they know they have met the Morrigan and soon will die. She gives and she takes away.

Perhaps the best-known tale of the Morrigan is to be found in the Irish epic called the *Tain bo Cuailgne* or "Cattle Raid of Cooley."[1] The great warrior Cuchulain was standing in the ford of a river, meeting all challengers in single combat. Favoring him, the Morrigan appeared as a beautiful young girl to offer him her body. When Cuchulain—who was too busy fighting to show much interest—refused her, she took a fierce revenge. She turned into an eel and wrapped herself around his foot as he stood fighting in the river. Cuchulain wounded the eel and continued his battle, cursing the Morrigan with the words: "You shall never be healed of your wound unless I myself heal you."

But the Morrigan wasn't finished. She turned herself into a cow and led a stampede of cattle through the river, right into Cuchulain. He wounded her again, cursed her again, and fought on. So she turned herself into a ravening wolf and attacked him. Again he wounded her, cursed her, and fought on.

Finally, worn out with his battles at the river, Cuchulain stepped aside to rest. He spied an old woman milking a cow. He longed for the sweet, cold milk, and the crone offered him a taste. He drank, and blessed her. She offered him another cup; he drank again, and blessed her again. She offered him yet a third; again he drank and blessed her.

The old woman then revealed herself as the Morrigan. By blessing her three times, Cuchulain had himself healed her of the three wounds. She turned into a raven and, screeching with laughter, flew away.

But the Morrigan has many faces. Though originally a goddess of Pagan Ireland, she reappears in medieval legend as Morgan le Fay, who has become a popular feminist icon, thanks to her starring role as Morgana in Marion Zimmer Bradley's well-known novel *The Mists of Avalon*.[2] Her name literally means "Morgana the Faery" and she is the quintessential sorceress of Arthurian mythology. In Thomas Malory's vast compendium of medieval Arthurian lore,[3] she is Arthur's wild and headstrong half-sister, brought up in a "nunnery" where she acquired the arts of "necromancy." Like the Morrigan, her power is associated with water, for she is part of that mysterious sisterhood called the Ladies of the Lake, a band of wise and magical women who dwell in the Isle of Avalon—which is but one more name for the old Celtic Otherworld.

In the old tales she is generally depicted as very beautiful, a delicate, dark-haired creature who draped her body in a shroud-like mantle of blue-black hue. Her magical powers were legendary, and she engaged in magical combat with her brother time and again, stealing his sword Excalibur and, after her plans were foiled, turning herself and her companions into standing stones in order to elude her pursuers. She dwells in the magical twilight midway between this world and the Otherworldly Avalon.

Her sexual nature is prodigious and, like her ancestress the Morrigan, she is not above mixing sexual desire with magic to work mischief among men. After enchanting Sir Lancelot, she threatens to kill him if he fails to choose a bedmate from among herself and three other queens. Lancelot remains loyal to Guinevere and in the end Morgan simply lets him go; similarly, and with heavy heart, she releases Ogier the Dane from mortal life despite her love for him.[4]

Because she is a Sorceress, because she has been to the Otherworld and back, she is not limited by ordinary social standards of conduct or ethics. She is asymmetrical, and simply doesn't care. Whether in mischief, magic, or healing, she is simply herself. One cannot call her immoral. Is a thunderstorm immoral because it rains down on our heads, or the wind evil when it bites us to the bone? Is a sunset "good" simply because we find it beautiful? Morgan is amoral, like a force of wild Nature—like the dark forest wherein she captures wanderers, or the deep lake wherein she and her wild sisters dwell.

If we examine the tempestuous Morgan along with her distant Pagan counterpart, the Morrigan, we may look deeply into the magic mirror of the Sorceress archetype. Let us begin in the most primal world of all, that of the animals. It is of the greatest importance to our purposes that the Irish Morrigan is a Raven Mother, and that this bird is her animal totem. Ravens belong to the bird family called *corvidae:* large, omnivorous, and gregarious to a degree verging on the obnoxious. These birds can't sing worth a lick, though their raucous blackbird language is quite communicative and extensive. Live food doesn't really interest them; they prefer dead things, like road-kill. They also have a taste for other birds' eggs. The fact that the fighting Celts would find ravens on the battlefield eating the rotting flesh of dead warriors must have added to the bird's mystique as totem spirit of the Morrigan.

Ravens also possess the wisdom aspect of the Life-and-Death Mother, and one of the most interesting things about them is their reaction to the death of a fellow raven. A raven will guard the dead body and rattle a death song, letting the other ravens know what has occurred. Soon they all form a circle about the corpse and dance round and round, croaking softly from deep within their throats.

It isn't hard to see why the ancient Celts associated the Morrigan with the raven. Considering the habits of the bird, it is easy to derive other connections also. For example, because its feathers are colored black, the raven calls to mind the beginning of all things, the maternal night, the primordial darkness and vital primal earth. Soaring through the sky in graceful, rag-winged flight, the raven is obviously a messenger. Some North American Indians and Siberian peoples once thought the raven to be the creator of the visible world; contemporary tribal peoples the world over still associate the raven with magic, believing that through the power of its spirit one can divine the future.[5]

The raven's association with death survived in medieval alchemy, where the raven appears as Saturn's bird, croaking to initiate the first stage of the alchemical process, the putrefaction or nigredo in which the aspirant is stripped of all affect, all previous assumptions, and plunged into that melancholy netherworld from whence rebirth may in time occur.

Finally, the raven is generally regarded, at least in folklore, as a solitary creature. This, perhaps, is a way of saying that although many are attracted to the mystic flame, few actually choose to leap into it to undergo the journey of separation from the real and visible world of the body.

Let us note that much of the Morrigan's power is drawn from rivers— she attacked Cuchulain as he stood in a river, and straddled a river herself when allowing the Dagda to enter her. Similarly, Morgan le Fay is one of the Ladies of the Lake, and pilots a magic barge back and forth between our world and the Otherworldly isle of Avalon. The Bone Goddess in her guise of Raven Mother, she who lies at the very root of the Wild Woman's soul, is also the spiritual water of life that fills the chalice of the Holy Grail.

This means that despite whatever illusions we may harbor regarding the extent of our evolutionary development, high or low, it's all the same; spiritual water will seep deep down into the nooks and crannies of the psyche, eroding all barriers and releasing the primal rivers of instinct and emotion. We may choose to jump farther down into the well as each canal lock is opened and more water gushes forth to overflow yet another sluice gate of our unrealized Self. Or we can stand on the edge of the abyss looking down the tunnel to a place where there is no beginning or end, only darkness—and fall in anyway.

Either way, once we are submerged within our own torrential depths, we may discover that spirit and flesh are one, that the symbolic raven who consumes the misconceptions in our souls is just the Morrigan, who eats the dessicated remains of our slain illusions.

Yet this process, this alchemical nigredo, is the road to healing and re-emergence. Another Bone Mother from yet another culture was an Aztec goddess with the tongue-twisting name of Tlazolteotl—it is simpler to approach her in translation and call her Filth Eater the Witch. A goddess of witchcraft and rampant sexuality, it was to her that dying Aztecs confessed their sins. She consumed those sins, just as the Morrigan consumes the dead remainders of our outworn selves. That's why she was called Filth Eater.

Again, the level that water finds when working as a spiritual element within human personality is emotional and instinctual in nature. This is why, as a woman spirals down into the emotional well of life and comes up again for air (the Hermetic symbol of the logical mind), she runs a gamut (or should we say gauntlet?) of feelings. Her maternal qualities may shift from nurturance, sympathy, and responsiveness to over-emotionalism, moodiness, and changeability. She may be open to transformation and regeneration but may also battle compulsive, self-destructive tendencies. Her muse may be sensitive, spiritual, creative, and imaginative, or delusional, vague, deceptive, and confused.

Never mind the narrow canyons and gorges, waterfalls, sand bars, cataracts, and rapids. Wherever the river of life might take her, a woman must learn to float, upstream or down, back and forth across its banks like a mist-enshrouded barge passing through the twilight, for the mystical lake of Arthurian legend, like the eternal rivers that empower the Morrigan, are symbols of the waters of the soul, and it is the business of a Sorceress to navigate those waters. Thus every woman who takes the path of the Sorceress is also a mistress of the separation of soul and body—the so-called witches of late medieval Europe, like all shamans, were skilled in traversing the astral realm. We may just as easily say, in the psychological sense, that all our dreams, creative flights of fantasy, and moments of inspiration also represent such a separation of soul and body. This form of Otherworld travel, whereby the soul is loosened from the shore of the body and conveyed by the wind of pure spirit, requires courage as well as an intense desire for discovery and change. Thus the spirit traveler is restless, hungry, a goal-less pursuer of dissatisfied longing, a dreamchaser seeking a wonder in a megalithic landscape fraught with illusion. Maybe she seeks comfort or runs from doting overcare. Perhaps, like the shamaness seeking a vision, the journey is an evolutionary one, a Grail quest that brings the spirit traveler from the primal womb of darkness to infinite light.

To travel in the spirit, then, is to seek with the eyes of the soul. Therefore the spirit traveler must remember that the water of the soul will always seek its own level.

If she is to become a Sorceress, that is. One way or another, every woman is a Sorceress.

The first prerequisite for being a Sorceress is to know your levels. This means becoming familiar with your own uncharted depths, your own internal river which is the path your soul will follow. Thus you will recognize your responses to ever-changing circumstance as well as your reactions to the responses of others. Knowing your levels, having the ability to feel and identify your emotions as empathetic tributaries reaching toward the various situations and conditions of the big river of life, gives you strength, makes you wise. It also enables you to dam up the gates and cut off the flow of watery emotions at will, so you may guide your feelings to flow in a direction of your own choosing.

If we are willing to choose our direction on the Silver Wheel of life— whether it be the eastern sunrise of the Warrior Woman, the western isles of the Lover, the warm southern summer of the Mother, or the wintry north of the Sorceress—then at the very least we will be operating from our rightful place of power when our time to greet the Morrigan arises.

A Sorceress or shamaness always operates from a position of power. A true shamaness knows her power spot, the place from which it is safe to journey into Otherworldly realms, whether to help herself or to help others recover from illness or injury. Within this circle of protective light, the shamaness experiences the center of her universe, that place inside her physical body from which her strength proceeds. Acutely aware of her supernatural senses, she is able to see, hear, taste, touch, and smell more clearly, more accurately, more perceptively, than before. Therefore we all must learn the location of our power place, both within the body and without, so that we can know where we are going and be less afraid when we get there. There are no excuses for being afraid.

Over time, women have explored the argument that little girls are taught to cry and be weak while little boys learn to be stoic and strong. Apologies to the psychotherapeutic community which holds that children are blank slates to be drawn upon by ignorant, abusive parents and/or relations, but the philosophy of magic holds that each of us enters life with our own agenda. Our parents and relations are only mirrors in which we may look to see the truth about ourselves and what we need to change.

Blank slate or not, so what? To hold the past responsible for our present reality is to allow the barge in which we float down the river of life to get stuck in the muddy shallows. If we hang on to the shadows of our childhood past, we shall never reach Avalon.

Furthermore, women have harped ad nauseam on the excuse that it is patriarchal society that holds them back. A sincere and heartfelt thank-you to the feminists who have brought about equal pay for equal work regardless of gender! But beyond such basic issues of human dignity, the battle of the sexes is likely to become an empty vendetta. Western women can no longer be controlled by outside oppression unless they allow it to happen. Yes, there will be attempts to placate or ignore us; we will still be abused, raped, and murdered (and so will men). But remember, the barge moves back and forth across the river, upstream or down; it does not sit banked on the shore, mired in the fetid swamplands. A woman need not wade in muck waiting for more shit to happen, for a woman who truly knows the Goddess knows freedom from all apparent limitations. Her thinking is magical. She does not worry and fester over the moral doings of society and its collective mindset. She does not wage her battle against the opposite sex. She stands against no one, because although she is able to function within the mundane, ordinary world, she knows she is not really part of it. She is subject to a different set of rules based on accessing personal power and self-knowledge. She has attained understanding of the principles of the Otherworld.

Thus a woman who knows is a true seeress fully in charge of her own destiny. She functions in the mundane world of cars and credit cards, of physics and chemistry. She moves easily between all worlds because she knows there is an Otherworld, and takes her sustenance, her fearlessness, and her vision from thence, and hence she realizes that the mundane world is dependent on the Otherworld for its existence.

She is aware that to open the doorway to the Otherworld is to allow the rules of that world to prevail over the mundane world, thus enabling her to alter her own reality, and thus she uses will, imagination, and courage in her daily life.

She recognizes the Goddess archetypes and their helpers (such as Rhiannon and her horse, Blodeuwedd and her owl, or Morrigan and her raven) as guardians, allies, guides, and advisors. She claims and uses her own innate power regardless of external circumstances and conditions, and thus she changes and dissolves outworn habits, values, limitations, and beliefs in order to re-create and transform her life.

She accepts that change comes slowly, and as a result of seeming chaos; therefore she forms clear goals and takes definite steps to make them happen.

She works to balance her mind, heart, and instincts. She enjoys and is grateful for life in all its wondrous forms, and she has a well-developed sense of the ridiculous which enables her to find humor in all things.

Exercise VI: Finding Your Power Place

As discussed above, everyone has a place of power, both inside themselves as well as outside, in particular physical locations on the earth. Such locations are an integral part of the Celtic Tradition—ancient holy places such as stone circles and barrow mounds play a major role in many legends and folktales, as do more purely natural holy places such as sacred trees and wells. There are many locations so powerful that their energy can be accessed by almost anyone; there are other places that are quite individual, and that may, perhaps, be powerful to you alone as vortices of energy linking your individuality to the Earth at large. Such locations are excellent for gathering empowerment, fine-tuning your thoughts or feelings, granting you the inspiration to become more creative, and healing your vulnerability to illness and depression.

This exercise can be performed indoors, although it is preferable to find a power place somewhere in Nature. You need no equipment, only yourself.

First, sit down and close your eyes. As in previous exercises, begin breathing deeply and feel your body, mind, and emotions completely relax. It is important to be calm and balanced when you find and identify your power place; its energizing influence will increase whatever emotions you may be feeling at the time.

When you feel peaceful, stand up. Begin walking, guided only by your feelings and the sensations of your body. Try to notice what part of your body is directing your movements. Follow its lead. Continue moving in this manner until you are pulled to a particular place. It will feel as if a magnet has drawn you to the spot.

Again, sit down, close your eyes, and just be. Allow any images, thoughts, emotions, and bodily sensations to wash over you like a dream. If you feel uncomfortable in any way, try to identify the source of your discomfort and let it go. Finally, locate and remember the area within your body that is particularly energized, alert, and aware at this time. This is your internal power place. It is from this place that you instinctually perceive the world.

Exercise VII: The Guardian Spirit Journey

Once you have found and identified your power place, you are ready to perform this exercise, which is similar to Exercise II, The Otherworld Journey. In this exercise, however, you are going to journey into the Otherworld guided by a goddess, with the intention of bringing something back. That "something" is your guardian spirit and can take any form, human or animal, plant or mineral, perhaps even an elemental entity such as an elf, gnome, or dwarf. If you wish to increase the benefits and intensity of the journey, perform it on your power place. (The same holds true for all the other exercises in this book.)

This exercise will show you a way to identify your goddess archetype and bring back this guardian spirit from the Otherworld. In order to make the journey, you will need the usual materials (a dark colored scarf or mask to cover your eyes, a rattle, a drum, and a friend to beat the drum).

As before, if you have no one to assist you in this exercise or would rather perform it alone, a cassette player and a recording of shamanic drumming will do as well.

As in Exercise II, find a quiet place (preferably your power spot) where you can remain undisturbed. Abstain from heavy food and drink for at least four hours before the exercise and wear loose, comfortable clothing.

If outdoors, you can achieve the darkness you need by tying the scarf over your eyes. If indoors, you may darken the room you have chosen and lie down flat on the floor. Have your friend sit with the drum in a corner of the room, or have the cassette recorder with the tape ready at your side. Do not time this journey. Let it take as long as is necessary to complete the process.

Once again, begin with deep and rhythmic breathing, proceeding with relaxation as before. When you are ready to begin your journey, state your intent. This time, you journey with the clear intention to bring back a guardian spirit.

Imagine your usual opening in the earth, be it a cave, barrow, a well, the bole of a tree, or an animal hole. Take your time, as always.

Now let your friend know that it's time to begin by shaking your rattle at a rhythm that you find comfortable. Have your friend follow the pace you set with the rattle. When you are ready to enter the earth, stop shaking your rattle but have your friend continue drumming in the same rhythm throughout the duration of the journey. If no one is assisting you in your journey, just wait until your picture of the Otherworld entrance is nice and clear, then reach over and turn on the cassette recorder.

Stand before the opening you have selected. Before you enter it, however, wait for your goddess archetype to appear. Maybe you know who she is; then again, you may be surprised at who shows up. If you have been working with the material in this book, your subconscious mind is very likely to respond by sending you an image of one of the Celtic goddesses such as Rhiannon, Arianrhod, or the Morrigan. But it is equally possible that you will respond to a very personal level of vision—you may just as easily produce an Athena or Aphrodite, a Yemanja or Kuan Yin figure. You may even meet with a goddess you don't recognize at all. (If this happens, try asking her what her name is. Once again, you may be surprised.)

Now allow the goddess to guide you into the entrance. Take her hand, ride on her back, do whatever it is she suggests and follow her instructions explicitly.

At some point you will emerge from the passage into a natural landscape. As usual, explore this natural setting in detail and remember that this time you are looking for something in particular, something to take back with you. Perhaps your goddess will accompany you in your search for a guardian spirit, or she may leave you to explore alone. This is okay. The main thing is to note all creatures that present themselves to you. The one you are to take back will show itself to you four times, in each of the four directions. Do not try to retrieve anything that does not exhibit this form of behavior.

Assuming that you have seen your guardian spirit and that it has shown itself to you four times, grab hold of it and embrace it. Then make your way back to the tunnel and call to your goddess, telling her that you are ready to return. She may show up to guide you back, you may just hear her voice in the distance, or your call may be met with silence. Whatever happens, return through the tunnel the way that you came, keeping your guardian spirit with you as you do so.

If have have not been able to retrieve anything, don't be discouraged. Simply wait a day or two and try again. If you have found your guardian spirit, you will experience a sense of joy, well-being, and renewed vitality. Maintain this renewed empowerment by spirit dancing your guardian at least once a week (see Exercise V).

Finally, write down your experience in your magical journal.

We have reached the end of our journey. The Silver Wheel, of course, has no end, but revolves eternally. This book, however, like all others, must come to the end of its course. Before departing, let us say a few more words about Morgan le Fay.

Morgan may be a creature of mischief, but she is also a figure of grandeur. In the medieval poem "Sir Gawain and the Green Knight," it is she, in her guise as the Crone, who orchestrates Gawain's seasonal combat for love of the Goddess—though in this poem it is she herself who is called "Morgan the Goddess."[6] Her grandeur arises, at least in part, from the fact that she is a healer. Let us not forget that it is she who, after so many battles with her brother Arthur, bears him away to Avalon in her magic barge to be healed of his wounds.

This, finally, is the ultimate gift of the Sorceress. She heals. And who is the recipient of her healing?

Antagonist, brother, hero, lover. We know who he is.

The battle of Camlann had been terrible. Mordred had been slain, at least, but Arthur now lay in a chapel nearby, direly wounded in the head. Only Sir Bedivere was left to him, and Bedivere had already taken the sword Excalibur and cast it into a lake by the chapel. There he had seen a wonder—a woman's pale hand had emerged from the lake, seized the sword, and borne it down beneath the water.

Now it was Arthur's turn.

Bedivere carried his lord to the lake, to the barge that waited by the banks. Three queens, veiled and robed in black, sat in the boat and wept.

"Lift me into the barge," commanded Arthur.

One of the queens, the most stately and regal of the three, placed Arthur's wounded head in her lap.

"My dear brother," she said to him, "you have stayed too long. The wound on your head is already cold."

And the barge began to slip away, over the fog-shadowed waters.

"My lord," called Bedivere, "do not desert me!"

"My time is past," came Arthur's voice, weakly from the fog. "I am going to Avalon."

The boat sailed on. Morgan wrapped her cloak about the crumpled body of Arthur, bringing azure-gray twilight to shade the eyes of her brother. She called upon the guardian spirits and helpers that served her. In green Avalon she would sing while sprinkling honeydew from exotic flowers over his gaping wounds. His fading light would be restored.

But for Bedivere, left behind on the lakeshore, there was only the wind in the sedge-grass, and the muting of swans as the boat faded away in the mist.

And then, at last, it disappeared....

Endnotes

1. Thomas Kinsella, translator, *The Tain.*

2. New York: Alfred A. Knopf, 1983.

3. Thomas Malory, *Le Morte D'Arthur,* ed. Keith Baines (New York: Mentor, 1962).

4. Thomas Bulfinch, *Bulfinch's Mythology* (New York: Avenel Books, 1978) 426-427, 689-692, 869.

5. J. E. Cirlot, *A Dictionary of Symbols* (New York: Philosophical Library, 1971), 71.

6. J. R. R. Tolkien, translator, *Sir Gawain and the Green Knight, Pearl and Sir Orfeo* (New York: Ballantine Books, 1980).

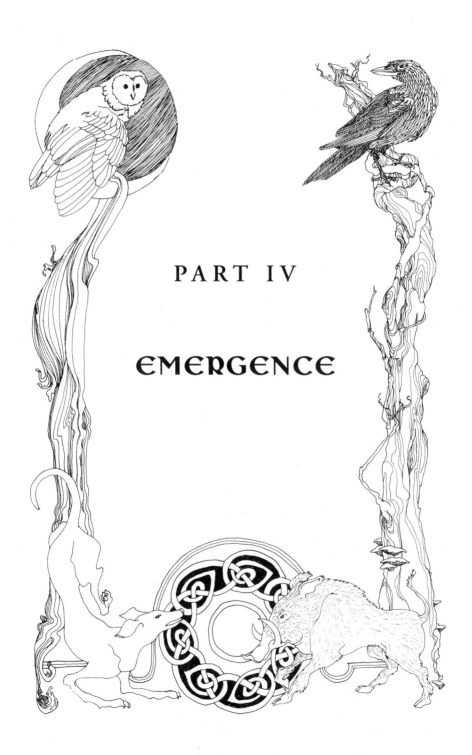

PART IV

EMERGENCE

EPILOGUE

THE MAIDEN APPEARED on the mound called Gorsedd Arberth. The night was bright with stars, the weather calm and fair, and the horse she rode whiter than the snowy peaks of the distant mountains. Her horse trod the ground at an even pace. Her garment of shining gold-brocaded silk was a glimmering halo about her slender form and her face was covered with a veil....

BIBLIOGRAPHY

Bedier, Joseph. *The Romance of Tristan and Iseult*, translated by Hilaire Belloc and Paul Rosenfeld. New York: Vintage Books, 1945.

Bloch, Dorothy. *"So the Witch Won't Eat Me": Fantasy and the Child's Fear of Infanticide*. Boston: Houghton Mifflin, 1978.

Bradley, Marion Zimmer. *The Mists of Avalon*. New York: Alfred A. Knopf, 1983.

Bulfinch, Thomas. *Bulfinch's Mythology*. New York: Avenel Books, 1978.

Cirlot, J. E. *A Dictionary of Symbols*. New York: Philosophical Library, 1983.

Coleridge, Samuel Taylor. "Kubla Khan," in W. H. Auden and Norman Holmes Pearson, eds., *Romantic Poets*. New York: Viking Press, 1969.

DeGrow, Rev. Katherine, and Dr. Teal Willoughby. Workshop material.

Deren, Maya. *Divine Horsemen: The Voodoo Gods of Haiti*. New York: Chelsea House Publishers, 1970.

Eliade, Mircea. *Shamanism: Archaic Techniques of Ecstasy*. Princeton: Princeton-Bollingen, 1972.

"Erik the Red's Saga," in *The Vinland Sagas: The Norse Discovery of America*, Magnus Magnusson and Herman Palssen, trans. Baltimore: Penguin, 1965.

Ford, Patrick, trans. *The Mabinogi*. Berkeley: University of California Press, 1977.

Fortune, Dion. *The Esoteric Philosophy of Love and Marriage*. New York: Samuel Weiser Inc., 1977.

Frazer, Sir James. *The Golden Bough*. New York: MacMillan Company, 1923.

Gantz, Jeffrey, trans. *Early Irish Myths and Sagas*. Harmondsworth: Penguin, 1981.

Gantz, Jeffrey, trans. *The Mabinogion.* London: Penguin, 1976.

Gimbutas, Marija. *The Goddesses and Gods of Old Europe,* Berkeley and Los Angeles: University of California Press, 1982.

Gimbutas, Marija. *The Language of the Goddess.* San Francisco: Harper and Row, 1989.

Graves, Robert. *The White Goddess.* New York: Farrar, Straus and Giroux, 1974.

Gray, John. *Men Are from Mars, Women Are from Venus.* New York: Harper Collins, 1992.

Heyn, Dalma. *The Erotic Silence of the American Wife.* New York: Turtle Bay Books, 1992.

Johnson, Kenneth and Marguerite Elsbeth. *The Grail Castle: Male Myths & Mysteries in the Celtic Tradition.* St. Paul, MN: Llewellyn Publications, 1995.

Johnson, Kenneth. *North Star Road: Shamanism, Witchcraft & the Otherworld Journey..* St. Paul, MN: Llewellyn Publications, 1996.

Jong, Erica. *Witches.* New York: Harry N. Abrams, 1981.

Jung, C. G. "Aion: Phenomenology of the Self," in *The Portable Jung,* Joseph Campbell, ed. Harmondsworth: Penguin, 1980.

Kennelly, Brendan, trans., ed. *The Penguin Book of Irish Verse.* Harmondsworth: Penguin, 1970.

Kinsella, Thomas, trans. *The Tain* (a translation of the Irish epic *Tain Bo Cuailnge).* Oxford: Oxford University Press, in association with The Dolmen Press, Dublin, 1979.

Leach, MacEdward, ed. *The Ballad Book.* New York: A. S. Barnes and Company, 1975.

Leland, Charles Godfrey. *Gypsy Sorcery and Fortune Telling.* New Hyde Park, NY: University Books, 1964.

Leonard, Linda Schierse. *Meeting the Madwoman.* New York: Bantam, 1993.

MacCana, Proinsias. *Celtic Mythology.* London: Hamlyn, 1973.

Mallory, J. P. *In Search of the Indo-Europeans.* London and New York: Thames and Hudson, 1994.

Malory, Thomas. *Le Morte D'Arthur,* Keith Baines, ed. New York: Mentor, 1962.

Matthews, Caitlin. *Arthur and the Sovereignty of Britain: King and Goddess in the Mabinogion.* London: Arkana, 1989.

Moore, Robert, and Douglas Gillette. *King, Warrior, Magician, Lover: Rediscovering the Archetypes of the Mature Masculine.* San Francisco: Harper San Francisco, 1990.

Murray, Margaret. *The God of the Witches.* London: Oxford University Press, 1970.

Perera, Sylvia Brinton. *Descent to the Goddess: A Way of Initiation for Women.* Toronto: Inner City Books, 1981.

Peterson, Gayle. *Birthing Normally: A Personal Growth Approach to Childhood.* Berkeley: Mindbody Press, 1984.

Rhys, John. *Celtic Folklore: Welsh and Manx,* 2 vols. London: Wildwood House, 1983.

Ross, Anne. *Pagan Celtic Britain.* London: Routledge & Kegan Paul, 1967.

Sasson, Jean. *Princess Sultana's Daughters.* New York: Doubleday, 1994.

Shuttle, Penelope and Peter Redgrove. *The Wise Wound: The Myths, Realities, and Meanings of Menstruation.* New York: Grove Press, 1988.

Talbot, Michael. *The Holographic Universe.* New York: HarperCollins, 1992.

Terr, Lenore, M. D. *Too Scared to Cry: Psychic Trauma in Childhood.* New York: Harper & Row, 1990.

Tolkien, J. R. R., trans. *Sir Gawain and the Green Knight, Pearl and Sir Orfeo.* New York: Ballantine Books, 1980.

Walton, Evangeline. *Island of the Mighty.* New York: Ballantine Books, 1975.

Whitmont, Edward C. *The Symbolic Quest.* New York: Harper & Row, 1973.

INDEX

Beroul, 36
birds
   crow, 94
   eagle, 67, 176
   hawk, 88, 154
   owl, 55, 57, 59, 61, 63, 65-69, 71, 73, 75, 77, 190
   raven, 68, 84, 86, 89, 94, 137, 148, 161, 184-187, 190
Blodeuwedd, 64-68, 84, 86, 99, 128, 131, 161, 190
blood, 11-13, 32-33, 39, 64, 66, 81, 137-138, 141, 167
Bobbit, Lorena, 70-71
Bobbit, John Wayne, 70-71
Bone Mother, 87-88, 94, 115, 128, 167-169, 171, 174, 181-183, 187
Borderline Personality Disorder (BPD), 146
Boyne River, 98, 184
Bradley, Marion Zimmer, 63, 184, 201
Bran, King, 57-58
Branwen, 36-37, 41, 57-60, 68, 75, 127-128
Brcs, 112
Brigid, St. Brigid's Day, 10, 114-115
Britain, 13, 44, 85, 102-103, 202-203
British Isles, 13-14, 45, 95, 148
Bronze Age, 167
Bui, 95
bulimia, 144
Bundy, Peg, 91, 142
burial mounds, 8
Burton, Tim, 169

Cad Goddeu (see Battle of the Trees)
Caer Arianrhod (see Arianrhod's Castle, Corona Borealis)
Camlann, Battle of, 194
Carterhaugh, 44-46, 48
Cassiopeia, 123
Cathbach, 64

Cattle Raid of Cooley, The, 64, 100, 184
cauldron of rebirth, 59
Celts, Celtic, 10-12, 15-17, 25, 33, 35-36, 38-40, 44, 49, 67-68, 84-87, 95, 98-99, 102-103, 112, 114-115, 123, 128, 131, 133, 146, 148, 156, 161-162, 169, 172, 176, 183, 185-186, 190, 192, 202-203, 207, 209, 213
Cerridwen, 67, 87-88, 94, 161
childbirth, 83, 85-86, 91, 101, 161
Chinese, 8, 32
Christianity, Christians, 8-9, 11, 15, 46, 63, 100, 114, 129, 148, 166, 208-209
Cigfa, 109, 112, 163-164
Cinderella, 58, 150-151, 169, 171
Clud, 43-44, 165
collective unconscious, 8-9, 46, 87, 113, 115, 145, 207
Conaire, King, 137-138
Connacht, 99
Connor of Ulster, King (also Connor mac Nessa), 33, 85, 99
Cormac mac Art, King, 35
corn dolly, 10
Cornwall, 36-37, 57, 68
Corona Borealis (see also Arianrhod's Castle), 10, 123
County Meath (Ireland), 95
Court of Don (see Cassiopeia)
Creirwy, 87
Crete, 171
Crone (archetype), 14-15, 18-19, 69-70, 85, 100, 102, 117, 149, 162, 170, 172, 181, 184, 193
Crunniuc, 85-86
Cuchulain, 64, 100, 184, 186
Culhwch, 98
Cynfael River, 66

Da Derga, 137-138
Dagda, 98, 184, 186
dance, dancing, 15, 65-66, 140, 159, 161-162, 169-177, 186
Danu, 95, 123, 183
death, 11, 13, 36-37, 59-60, 66-71, 75, 78-79, 81, 84-88, 90, 92, 94, 98, 100-102, 115, 131, 133, 137-138, 146, 149-150, 152, 161, 167, 175, 181, 183, 186
Deirdre, 32-34, 37, 39, 41-42, 57, 85
Demon Lover, 38, 42, 44-46, 51, 168-175
depression, 72, 83, 100, 145-146, 190
Destruction of Da Derga's Hostel, The, 137-138
Dinas Station, 132
Dion, Celine, 70, 133
Dithorba, 99
Divine Child (see also Mother, Divine), 98, 166-167
Don (see also Danu), 20, 38, 62, 73-74, 82, 95, 123-124, 126, 128-129, 132, 146, 153, 161, 173-175, 183, 192-193
double rose, 45
dreams, 9-10, 38, 44, 46, 90, 111, 113, 142-143, 147, 168, 172-174, 187
Druids, 83, 129
drums, drumming, 118-120, 175-176, 191-192
Dyaus, 168
Dylan, 125, 130-131
Dyved, 5, 42, 81, 94, 100, 109

Earth, 10-11, 13, 15, 45-46, 64-65, 75, 84, 95, 97, 99, 112, 114, 119, 123, 128, 131, 140-141, 147, 152, 154, 161-162, 168, 170, 176-177, 181, 186, 190, 192
Edward Scissorhands (film), 169
Elaine of Astolat, 60

Elan, 132
Eleanor of Aquitaine, 33
Elfland, Queen of, 148, 150
elves, 45-46, 148-150
Emain Macha, 86, 95, 99
empowerment, 39-40, 57, 69, 94, 99-101, 117, 126, 143, 152, 190, 193
Epona, 14, 86
Ereshkigal, 167
eros, 9, 31, 39, 57, 113, 171-172
Europe, medieval, 148, 187
Evnissyen, 58-60
Excalibur, 185, 194

fairytales, 38, 119
Fiana, 35
Filth Eater (Tlazolteotl), 187
fish (salmon), 88, 98, 114
Fisher King, 112-113, 207
Florida, 71
Fomorians, 112
France, 12, 33
Freya, 68, 147-148

Galatea, 71
Gaul, Gauls, 12, 98
Gawain, 63, 72-73, 97, 193, 195, 203
geis (geissa), 34-35
Gimbutas, Marija, 68, 78, 102, 168, 202
Gloucester, 98
Goddess
    battle goddess, 85-86
    Bone Goddess, 186
    Dark Goddess, 141, 152, 162, 166-168, 171-172, 183
    Death Goddess, 68-71, 79, 84-87, 92, 94, 98, 101-102
    Goddess Era, 15
    Goddess of the Land, 79, 81, 83, 85, 87, 89, 91, 93, 95, 97, 99, 101, 103, 123, 183

Stay in Touch...

Llewellyn publishes hundreds of books on your favorite subjects!
On the following pages you will find listed some books now available on related subjects. Your local bookstore stocks most of these and will stock new Llewellyn titles as they become available. We urge your patronage.

ORDER BY PHONE

Call toll-free within the U.S. and Canada, 1–800–THE MOON.
In Minnesota call (612) 291–1970.
We accept Visa, MasterCard, and American Express.

ORDER BY MAIL

Send the full price of your order (MN residents add 7% sales tax) in U.S. funds to:
Llewellyn Worldwide
P.O. Box 64383, Dept. K371–9
St. Paul, MN 55164–0383, U.S.A.

POSTAGE AND HANDLING

- ◆ $4.00 for orders $15.00 and under
- ◆ $5.00 for orders over $15.00
- ◆ No charge for orders over $100.00

We ship UPS in the continental United States. We cannot ship to P.O. boxes. Orders shipped to Alaska, Hawaii, Canada, Mexico, and Puerto Rico will be sent first-class mail.
International orders: Airmail—add freight equal to price of each book to the total price of order, plus $5.00 for each non-book item (audiotapes, etc.). Surface mail—add $1.00 per item.
Allow 4–6 weeks delivery on all orders. Postage and handling rates subject to change.

GROUP DISCOUNTS

We offer a 20% quantity discount to group leaders or agents. You must order a minimum of 5 copies of the same book to get our special quantity price.

FREE CATALOG

Get a free copy of our color catalog, *New Worlds of Mind and Spirit*. Subscribe for just $10.00 in the United States and Canada ($20.00 overseas, first-class mail). Many bookstores carry *New Worlds*—ask for it!

The Grail Castle
MALE MYTHS & MYSTERIES IN THE CELTIC TRADITION
Kenneth Johnson & Marguerite Elsbeth

Explore the mysteries that lie at the core of being male when you take a quest into the most powerful myth of Western civilization: the Celtic-Teutonic-Christian myth of the Grail Castle.

The Pagan Celtic culture's world view—which stressed an intense involvement with the magical world of nature—strongly resonates for men today because it offers a direct experience with the spirit often lacking in their lives. This book describes the four primary male archetypes—the King or Father, the Hero or Warrior, the Magician or Wise Man and the Lover—which the authors exemplify with stories from the Welsh *Mabinogion,* the Ulster Cycle and other old Pagan sources. Exercises and meditations designed to activate these inner myths will awaken men to how myths—as they live on today in the collective unconscious and popular culture—shape their lives. Finally, men will learn how to heal the Fisher King—who lies at the heart of the Grail Castle myth—to achieve integration of the four archetypal paths.

1–56718–369–7, 224 pp., 6 x 9, illus., softcover　　　　　　　　**$14.95**